CAMBRIDGE LIBRARY COLLECTION

Books of enduring scholarly value

Polar Exploration

This series includes accounts, by eye-witnesses and contemporaries, of early expeditions to the Arctic and the Antarctic. Huge resources were invested in such endeavours, particularly the search for the North-West Passage, which, if successful, promised enormous strategic and commercial rewards. Cartographers and scientists travelled with many of the expeditions, and their work made important contributions to earth sciences, climatology, botany and zoology. They also brought back anthropological information about the indigenous peoples of the Arctic region and the southern fringes of the American continent. The series further includes dramatic and poignant accounts of the harsh realities of working in extreme conditions and utter isolation in bygone centuries.

Across Iceland

Although he was a member of the Royal Geographical Society, and author of a number of books on geography, little is known of William Bisiker. Published in 1902, this is an account of an expedition, led by him, across central Iceland in 1900. The five men and one woman journeyed from the north-east of the country down to the south-west, and the book also gives accounts of visits to the Faroe Islands and coastal journeys to the fjords. Including maps, photographs and an extensive appendix compiled by expedition member and botanist Arthur William Hill on the island's plant life, this work remains a detailed and engaging portrait. The impressions made upon the party by natural features such as geysers, quicksand and lava formations are vividly described, as are the visits to isolated settlements and farms. The chapter on Reykjavik covers the political situation in the country, still under Danish rule.

Across Iceland

With Illustrations and Maps, and an
Appendix on the Plants Collected

WILLIAM BISIKER
A.W. HILL

CAMBRIDGE
UNIVERSITY PRESS

CAMBRIDGE
UNIVERSITY PRESS

University Printing House, Cambridge, CB2 8BS, United Kingdom

Cambridge University Press is part of the University of Cambridge.
It furthers the University's mission by disseminating knowledge in the pursuit of
education, learning and research at the highest international levels of excellence.

www.cambridge.org
Information on this title: www.cambridge.org/9781108079853

This edition first published 1902
This digitally printed version 2017

ISBN 978-1-108-07985-3 Paperback

ACROSS ICELAND

THE CAMP AT HVERAVELLIR.

ACROSS ICELAND

BY

W. BISIKER, F.R.G.S.

WITH ILLUSTRATIONS AND MAPS

AND

AN APPENDIX BY A. W. HILL, M.A., ON THE PLANTS COLLECTED

LONDON

EDWARD ARNOLD

Publisher to the India Office

1902

CONTENTS

LIST OF ILLUSTRATIONS

ix

LIST OF MAPS

CHAPTER I

THESE notes, besides describing a journey made during the summer of 1900 across Central Iceland from the north-east to the south-west, give an account of further travels by land in the west, and by sea along the coast and into the fjords of the north-west, north and east coasts.

The voyage to Iceland was made in one of the vessels owned by the United Steamship Company, a Danish company trading from Copenhagen to Leith, and thence to the Faroes and Iceland.

We were six in all—a semi-scientific party. There was Miss J. A. Hastie, a woman who has travelled much in Europe, Asia, Africa, and America, and who is not unacquainted with our Colonies at the Antipodes, or with the islands of the South Seas. She was specially interested in the botany of the country, in its folk-lore, and in the people. Then there was Captain W. H. Cope; he had been at sea for the greater part of his life, and had in the course of his journeyings seen much of the world; he was our nautical adviser, and we referred to him in

matters connected with the sea. W. Glen, Miss
Hastie's cousin, was known as the "handy man"
of the party. If anybody was in difficulties, Glen
was always on the spot to lend a helping hand. He
produced all sorts of things at the right moment.
Did any one require a screw-driver, then Glen had it ;
want a corkscrew, Glen could supply it ; a pair of
scissors, he produced them—some string, a strap, it
was all the same. If a camera struck work, Glen
could render the strike ineffective, for he carried two,
and could lend one without interfering with his own
photographic work. A. W. Hill, of King's College,
Cambridge, was our botanist—who describes what he
saw. H. H. Thomas, of Balliol, paid special attention
to the geological formation of the country that we
traversed, and he was frequently to be seen, camera
in hand, taking shots at interesting formations—a
glaciated lava surface, a volcanic vent, or an immense
"erratic" boulder or "perched block," for instance ;
he also sketched industriously, and sometimes paced
the ground compass in hand in order that he might
record in his note-book the direction of a line of
fissure, or the position of hot springs along that
line; or something else of interest to geologists in
particular. I was the geographer, whose mission it
was to make a map of a small portion of the country
traversed, to get a general idea of its conformation,
and to note valleys and mountains, ice-fields and
snow slopes, lava flows and hot springs, mighty
rivers and tiny rivulets. I undertook to chronicle
the events of the journey and to "take shots"—
photographic shots—at men and things. We were
all more or less devoted to sport, and frequently the

desire to kill took possession of us, especially when
we caught sight of duck, grouse, or golden plover—
or, when we came to stream or river where trout or
salmon were known to abound, we had a desire to
cast a fly. But it was maddening to know that our
desires could not be gratified, for where were gun
and cartridges, rod and line? The man who had
undertaken to look after that branch of our preliminary arrangements had failed us at the last
moment, and it was not till too late, when we
were embarking at Leith, that we learned that he
was not coming with us. It was not his fault, poor
fellow, but his misfortune. He had come a cropper
from his bicycle, falling on his head, had remained
unconscious for more than twelve hours, and had
been forbidden by his medical advisers to travel—
all this we knew nothing of until we were embarking
at Leith, when it was altogether too late to procure
another sporting outfit to replace that which we had
fondly believed to be already on board ship, but
which was really lying many miles away, far beyond
our reach. But I will hasten over a subject that
awakens the most tantalising of recollections, for
many were the opportunities that were missed.

One Saturday in June 1900 we embarked upon
the steam-ship *Ceres*, and early in the afternoon set
sail from Leith on our voyage North. All the
morning the weather had been fine, and it promised
to continue so before we started, but we had scarcely
reached the open sea before we entered a fog, which
increased in denseness as we progressed. As a consequence the steam-whistle was sounded every few
minutes, much to the discomfiture of many of the

passengers on board ; but Miss Hastie seemed to rise
above such petty annoyances, for she took her seat on
deck immediately beneath the whistle, and this spot
was her resort during the whole voyage, notwithstand-
ing the fact that the fog continued at intervals for
the greater part of the journey, and that the steam-
whistle frequently made day hideous with its noise.
Conversation with her when the fog was densest was
difficult, for it was punctuated—very incorrectly as a
rule—by the shrill blasts that broke in suddenly and
without warning, often causing the thread of a
discourse to be lost, or an interrupted remark to
fall flat on being completed, or perhaps repeated,
when silence once more reigned.

As a result of the fog we proceeded at half speed
only, and during the night the whistle was most
aggressive, causing one's slumbers to be somewhat
broken. In my own case the steam - whistle was
not the only disturbing influence at night, for my
cabin companion had a noisy way of enjoying the
repose of the just, and often the intervals between
the blasts were filled in with sounds that resembled
the rumbling of thunder, and not very distant
thunder either.

The second day out was a repetition of the first
as regards fog, progress made, shrill whistling, etc.
The vessel glided on slowly and smoothly, and we
employed the time, when not eating and drinking, in
the way usual at sea—by reading, chatting with our
fellow - passengers, and comparing notes of former
travels, varied now and then by a " rubber," or a
stroll on deck for exercise. Meals were served at the
following hours : 8 A.M., coffee and rusks ; 10 A.M.,

breakfast; 3 P.M., dinner—the chief meal of the day; 8 P.M., supper. At breakfast and supper there were many dishes of smoked, uncooked food—fish, meats, sausages, etc. ; but the members of our party did not take very kindly to these uncooked delicacies, and they were left for those who relished them—the Danes, Germans, and passengers of other nationalities, of whom there were many on board.

The fog cleared in the evening and the South Ronaldshay light was sighted. Several members of our party looked with no little interest at the headland, especially our nautical adviser, Captain Cope, for he had had a very unpleasant and dangerous experience thereabouts only two months before : he had been wrecked not far from it in the Shetland steamer, the *St. Rognvald*, which broke up and became a total loss. The vessel struck in the middle of the night, and he escaped in a very light and airy costume, consisting of a suit of pyjamas and an overcoat.

Next morning the weather was remarkably clear and bright until breakfast time, when we entered other fog banks and remained more or less in them until late in the afternoon ; but on nearing our first port of call we emerged into clear weather.

CHAPTER II

THE first sight of the Faroes was impressive. The
bold outlines of the islands were well-marked features.
The dip (or tilt) of the ancient lava flows could be
traced from one island to another. A dome-shaped
block, Lille Dimon, was the most striking island,
while the almost perpendicular escarpments of Skuo
stood as evidence of the power of the stormy Atlantic,
whose seas continually beat at the base of the cliffs.

Trangisvaag, in the island of Sudero, was the first
port of call. In the fjord leading to it the cloud-
effects were many and very fine. As the warm, moist
air coming in from the sea was carried against the
cool faces of precipitous lava mountains, so the
moisture condensed and swept along their sides, at
times completely hiding the highest points from view ;
but the effects were ever-changing. Fine specimens
of jointed basalt are these mountains ; flow upon flow
can be traced for miles in almost horizontal parallel
lines. But little vegetation is to be seen—the total
absence of trees, a little grass, and much peat moss
are the features that first appeal to one who is not a
botanist.

Ashore one is first struck with the Faroese themselves : they are a fine race, and retain their native
politeness and independence of character ; they are
courteous in the extreme to strangers. Most of the
men are fishermen or sailors, and many, through their
consequent contact with English-speaking people, can
converse in good understandable English. A small
trade is done in wool, and we met two of the islanders,
fine types of the race, returning from their day's
work ; they were quite picturesque figures, for,
besides being attired in the national costume, they
had wound round them a quantity of wool, which in
these islands is generally plucked, not shorn, from
the sheep's back. The national costume consists of a
sort of brewer's cap, having red and blue stripes as a
rule, a cloth tunic, a waistcoat, and knee breeches
split at the knees, but very rarely buttoned, rough
woollen stockings and skin shoes. The fishermen
often dispense with tunic and waistcoat, and wear in
their place a woollen jersey with long sleeves, that has
a strong sheepy smell, having a particular pattern
worked in pale blue and red on a white ground. The
women I saw wore dresses of white striped cotton
stuff, no ordinary head covering, but shawls across
the shoulders, which were often pulled over the head,
and wooden clogs on the feet.

All the buildings at Trangisvaag are built of wood
so far as the superstructure is concerned, the sub-
structure often being made of blocks of basalt. The
roofs of the oldest buildings are covered with grass ;
the bark of the silver birch is put on the rafters,
which is then turfed over, the grass as a rule growing
luxuriantly during summer—thus are the roofs made

water-tight. The most modern houses are covered with galvanised iron, but as they are not numerous the town is decidedly picturesque. There are several ancient-looking wooden buildings, the church being one of the oldest, with a record of fifty years.

I have stated that most of the male population are fishermen, consequently the chief trade of the islands is in fish — cod-fish. The fish, as soon as brought to land, are cut open by women (who all work at this industry also); they are then washed in water, sometimes sea-water and sometimes fresh, and stacked in heaps with plenty of salt between the layers. They remain so for perhaps three months, covered with tarpaulins held down by heavy lumps of basalt. When properly salted the fish are washed and spread on a floor laid with slabs of basalt. When dry, the fish are stored in sheds, where they are packed in bales ready for export to Spain or Italy, which are the chief markets for salted cod.

The town of Trangisvaag is on the northern side of the fjord at the base of high weather-worn basaltic crags, which frown down upon it and form a grand background. There is a quantity of peat moss on the slopes at the foot of these mountains, often scored deeply by the numerous watercourses.

At Trangisvaag it was quite evident that we were approaching the Arctic circle, for at midnight there was light enough for the houses and other objects on shore to be seen from the vessel's deck, half a mile distant, and to enable me to write up notes without the aid of artificial light.

We steamed out of Trangisvaag fjord in the early morning, but as the weather was dull and cloudy we could not see much of the small islands, Lille Dimon (Little Diamond) and Store Dimon (Great Diamond), for they were cloud-capped and otherwise much obscured by drifting clouds. A few hours later we anchored opposite to Thorshavn in the island of Stromo, the capital and chief town of the Faroes.

IN THORSHAVN (FAROES).

Thorshavn is a very quaint and picturesque place, and many are the peculiar buildings and dwellings in the heart of the town, where the streets are very narrow indeed. No general plan has been followed in the laying out of the town, for the streets run in all directions, up and down hill, and along valleys or depressions in the ground. The styles of architecture are various—a single-storied picturesque shanty of ancient style, with grass-covered roof, having

opposite to it a pretentious modern building roofed
with galvanised iron, which rises high above, its three
stories quite overshadowing the humble neighbour.
These turf and grass-grown roofs are a feature in the
appearance of the town.   The general absence of
trees is striking, though one notices with something
of surprise the almost tropical luxuriance of foliage in
some of the gardens that are more or less sheltered
from the strong winds which so frequently sweep over
the islands.   The only tree I saw there worthy of the
name was a sycamore in the front garden of a very
picturesque cottage standing on a rather elevated site
in the middle of the town.

We had not all brought oilskins, so Thomas and
I visited several stores in the course of a search for
some—at one of them they had coats only for sale,
at another there were nether garments and sou'-
westers in addition, but oh, how oily they were, and
sticky! and how smelly!   Had we purchased, no
doubt it would have added to our safety when
crossing ice-fields or lava flows, or when ascending
snow slopes, for we should undoubtedly have found
ourselves stuck fast to saddles on the occasions when
the ponies were endeavouring to get rid of us by
their frequent stumbles.   But we would have none
of the oily, sticky, and smelly garments.

I strolled about, camera in hand, and found that
many of the women and girls were quite anxious to
be photographed; at one spot I came upon a group
of women squatting on the ground; as I approached,
several others hastened to join the group, at the
same time inviting me to photograph them, which
I did.   Shortly afterwards my films came to an end,

so I made a journey to the *Ceres*, which was lying at
anchor half a mile from the shore, in order to reload
the camera.

I engaged two young Faroese to row me to the
vessel, and on arrival enjoined them to await me
that they might put me ashore again; when, however, I had changed the films and was ready to
return, they were nowhere to be found—the young
beggars had gone off with another fare, and had left
me to my own devices and to the off chance of a
"lift" in another boat. I felt much inclined to
make a murderous attack upon the Queen's English,
to say nothing of the young Faroese had they come
my way while pacing the deck in impotent wrath;
but I was obliged to restrain myself, for there was no
one with whom I could with justice quarrel, so I
suppressed the rising ire, and went in search of somebody who could speak my native language. In the
end I found a Faroese with some knowledge of
English, and arranged for a passage in a cargo-boat
then about to return to the shore. Soon I was being
conveyed from the *Ceres* at the rapid rate—for a
very heavily laden cargo-boat, that is—of about a
knot an hour. However, I reached the shore in due
course, just in time to join our party at lunch at the
hotel, where they were being entertained by a fellow-
passenger. A merry meal we had, and in the course
of it our host joined us in criticising the appoint-
ments of the table, but, in spite of a few makeshifts,
they were not at all bad, and the meal itself was
decidedly good.

The voyage to Klaksvig was of much interest, for
our course lay in channels between islands and in

fjords. The formation of the basaltic hills was most striking, the many pyramidal shapes impressing us greatly. There were numerous dykes in the mountain side, deep ravines scored perpendicularly in the basaltic formation, where softer intrusive material had been eroded more rapidly than the rock on each side. At the entrance to Kalsofjord (the channel between the islands of Kalso on the west and Bordo and Kuno on the east side) there was a very strong current flowing against us in a southerly direction; a course was therefore steered close in-shore to avoid the full strength of the current in mid-stream. Klaksvig lies in a bay in the island of Bordo, and to reach it a turn has to be made eastward between the islands of Kuno and Bordo. At the entrance to the bay anchor was dropped, and there we remained all night. We were close to the southern end of the island of Kuno, where a very fine specimen of a pyramidal mountain frowned down upon us from the height of nearly 2300 feet—it is a pyramid that might well cause the shade of Cheops, if ever passing that way, to hide his diminished head and fade into oblivion. We witnessed some very fine cloud-effects in the course of the journey to Klaksvig, for the clouds drifting over the high hills often streamed away far to leeward of them.

During the voyage I often wrote my notes somewhere about midnight, and this night, while thus employed in my cabin, my "stable companion" took it into his head that I was preventing him from the proper enjoyment of his slumbers, and growled out something to that effect; so, to avoid raising his wrath, I interrupted the course of the

notes and turned in; but it was not to sleep, for
I had scarcely laid head upon pillow before certain
sounds from the bunk below made it evident that
unconsciously he was going to turn the tables upon
me, and that, by stertorously enjoying his slumbers,
he would prevent me from peacefully enjoying mine.
After several ineffectual attempts to stop the snoring,
I at last fled to the saloon, far out of range of the
noise, and there reposed in peace for the rest of the
night.

At Klaksvig Miss Hastie, Hill, Thomas, and
myself went ashore. We hunted the "lions" in
couples: Miss Hastie going off with Hill to seek
specimens first of all, while Thomas and I were bent
on making a trial survey of the bay of Klaksvig,
just to keep our hands in. We did this before
visiting the "lions," which here assume the shape
of whales, or rather whales' skulls, a number of
which have been built up so as to form a dividing
wall between two properties. On one side of this
wall there is a cod-liver oil factory, which we inspected;
it was not quite so smelly as are some factories where
shark or whale oil is produced—but more of that
anon! One of the vats was full of a rich brown
liquid, which we were informed was unrefined cod-
liver oil. The oil is exported in that state after
being run into casks, many of which were strewed on
the hillside. A pretty picture was seen near the
wharf, where several young women were busily
engaged washing cod-fish in a bath under cover of
an open shed. A portion of the town of Klaksvig
is built on a narrow strip of land that separates
Klaksvig bay from Borovig bay—a strip that has

been formed partly of moraine debris, and partly by
the silting up of shingle by the sea.   Facing Borovig
bay there is a row of boat-sheds that are peculiar in
that they are built of boulders in a small break in
the sloping shore, and that the roofs are formed of
smaller boulders laid upon a wooden framework.
The roofs did not seem capable of keeping out much
rain, and doubtless they were not built for that
purpose, but for keeping out the snow during winter
when the boats are laid up.

In the evening we left Klaksvig and proceeded
into Kalsofjord, past the great pyramid; but its
lofty head was under a cloud, so we could not admire
its full proportions.   Passing up the fjord the atmosphere cleared, and one could not help being much
struck with the grandeur of the scenery.   High
precipitous mountains rose up on each side of the
fjord; at a first glance, one would say that there
was very little land at their foot suitable for cultivation, or for grazing purposes, so near to the water's
edge did the mountains seem; but we saw many
farms there, and several villages, picturesque places
with quaint-looking buildings, nestling in hollows at
the base of the hills.   What soil there is must be
very prolific, judging from the population settled on
it.   On the west side, and near to the north end of
the fjord, there are some very fine specimens of
common basaltic land forms—two grand corries,
a fine dyke, some sheer faces of rock, and as we
passed by the end of the land an almost sheer
precipice which faced west came into view, while
standing out at its foot there was a solitary basaltic
column.   When coming up the fjord the steam-

whistle was frequently sounded in order that we might hear the very fine echoes for which it is noted; the interval is a long one, some three or four seconds. At the corries the sound echoed and re-echoed until it finally died away in the heights above.

On emerging from the fjord and putting out to sea, we encountered a slight swell from the west, so the vessel rolled a bit; it was really not much, but being the first time during the voyage, it was much disliked by those who were not proof against *mal de mer*. The clear atmosphere was soon left behind, for we entered another fog bank when only a few miles distant from the land. At once the music (!) of the steam-whistle was resumed, and our ears were again tortured by its shrill blasts.

CHAPTER III

NEXT day rain, fog, and mist prevailed, so there was much whist-playing and smoking below, and much blowing of whistle above. Towards evening we were off the coast of Iceland; the land was not visible, for we were enveloped in fog, but there was no doubt about it, for we could *hear* that land was not far distant. It may seem strange, but it was a fact, we were really feeling our way along the coast by the aid of the steam-whistle. The land thereabouts rises abruptly from the sea, and the echoes from the sheer faces of rock enabled the officers of the vessel to judge their distance. We went dangerously near to another vessel in the fog, but soon afterwards it cleared off a bit, and there, just abeam on the starboard side, was the other vessel, sufficiently close to be a dangerous neighbour in thick weather. At midnight we were going full speed ahead, but when I awoke at seven in the morning it was to find that our experiences of fog were not at an end, that we were again in a very dense one, and that we were lying-to. After breakfast it lifted sufficiently to allow of a course being shaped for Northfjord, our first port of call in Iceland. Much of the scenery of this fjord was obscured by the thick atmosphere, but occasional glimpses through rifts proved that we were missing many fine scenes that are on view when the conditions are favourable. The first sight of Iceland was obtained at Dalatangi Point, four or five miles to the north of the entrance to Northfjord. In the fog we had gone too far north. Other glimpses on the way were of a corrie near Dalatangi, and the face of the mountains near Mjofifjord. Our stay at North-fjord was of but short duration, and there was no time to go ashore, so the only view we had of the town was obtained from the vessel's deck.

We had a number of Faroese passengers on board, bound for various ports in Iceland ; they were good types of the race, and I obtained permission to photograph some of them.

Seythisfjord was not far distant, and in a few hours we were steaming up the fjord towards the town at its head. The scenery and geological structure of these fjords were similar to what we had passed through two days before in the Faroes. Towards the head of the fjord there are many waterfalls on the mountain-sides ; in fact, it is a district of waterfalls, for there are some fine ones up the valley, where a fair-sized river and its various tributaries rush down from all sides in a series of great leaps and bounds over ledges of rocks fifty, sixty, a hundred feet high, finally joining and tumbling over the lowest ledge in a grand cascade (which I photographed) to the river below—the "valley of waterfalls" would be a descriptive name to bestow upon it.

It was at Seythisfjord that we first set foot upon

the soil of Iceland. We were conveyed to the shore by the steam-launch and boats from a man-of-war, the Danish guardship, that was lying in the harbour. We were so honoured because the captain of our vessel was an officer in the Danish Navy, and it was intended as an attention to him. It seems that some of the vessels belonging to the Company are captained by officers of the Navy, who are appointed to the command by the Danish authorities as a sort of reward for services, for during their term — three years, I think—they draw their pay as officers of the Navy in addition to what is due to them from the Company.

On shore our party split up as usual, Miss Hastie and Hill going off in search of plants, while the "Nautical Adviser," Thomas, and I wandered along the sea-shore and into the town. We were pestered by an Icelander having a very crude idea of the English language who had been imbibing the "lemonade" of the country, and if he had not "three sheets in the wind," at least there was one little sheet flapping about, the end of which was flicking at us at inconvenient moments. We tried to shake him off, but it was of no avail. He had a notion that we wanted a guide to conduct us into the interior of Iceland, and he claimed to be very competent and to know everything of the country. We did not doubt his competency, or if so we did not inform him, but tried to make him understand that we had made our arrangements for guidance, and that the men we had engaged were teetotallers. For a long while he dogged our footsteps, and it was not until we had got clear of the town and were

making tracks up the valley towards the waterfalls
that we lost him. On the way we joined Miss Hastie
and Hill, who seemed quite satisfied with the result
of their grubbing amongst what—to those of us at
least who had not been educated botanically—looked
like very common weeds. Together we slowly, very
slowly, made our way up the valley, for there were
many stoppages while plants were being dug out
and transferred to small tin boxes that looked like
tobacco tins—indeed, I think they were originally
intended to hold the " weed " of the smoker and not
" Weeds—various." So much time was occupied by
these stoppages, that at last it became a question
whether we should be able to reach the lowest and,
as we believed, the finest of the waterfalls, for we
were expected to be on board at a certain time, in
readiness for departure ; the question was much
debated, and there seemed to be a general desire to
discuss the matter rather than to make the attempt
to reach the fall. I determined to try, and was
informed that I should miss the steamer.

I could see the misty spray rising from the fall
not a mile distant, so I set out across swamps and
peat bogs, caring but little for such trifles, for I had
resolved to see that fall. Well, I *did* reach the fall,
and after photographing it, crossed the river just
below it, and returned on the other side of the valley.
It was a rather difficult journey, for I had a severe
cross-country course to cover, with a number of fairly
long jumps over the mountain streams on the way,
but, nevertheless, I reached the *Ceres* half an hour
before the other members of the party. Then,
strange to say, none of them seemed to believe that

I had reached the waterfall at all ; but the photograph
of it is the best evidence that I can offer in support
of my contention that I did.

The soil at Seythisfjord looked very good, and
would doubtless yield good crops were the summer a
bit longer and the ripening power of the sun rather
stronger.   There is much peat and boggy land on

THE WATERFALL, SEYTHISFJORD.

the slopes below the steep escarpments on each side
of the fjord, and in the river-flats up the valley ;
many ponies are grazed here, and as some of the
boggy land is being drained by deep dykes, the
number is likely to increase ; the peat that is removed
in cutting the dykes is built up at their sides to
form dividing fences.

The valley at the head of Seythisfjord is a fine
specimen of the result of sub-aerial erosion, for its

form is due to the denuding action of frost and snow, wind and rain, storm and sunshine. There is a vast corrie at the head, which is shelved in a series of steps right down to the flat through which the river meanders. It is at these shelves or ledges of the harder strata that the waterfalls and cascades already mentioned are to be found—there, where the river and its branches rush over the edge of one terrace and plunge down to the next.

This being our first experience of the Icelanders, our attention was attracted by the peculiar head-dress worn by the women, which is common to all classes—a small black knitted cap, about four or five inches in diameter, from which a silver tube hangs suspended at the side of the head; through the tube is strung a number of cords or silken threads that hang down as a tassel.

We ought to have sailed late in the evening, but a thick fog settled over the land and prevented a start. Wonderful echoes can be produced at Seythis-fjord; the steam-whistle was sounded several times, and the sound echoed and re-echoed again and again, the reverberation continuing for many seconds before it died away in the distance among the mountain tops. Fog and misty rain continued through the night and well into the small hours of the morning; but at about five o'clock it lifted sufficiently to allow the *Ceres* to put to sea. Progress was slow, and the frequent blasts of the steam-whistle that disturbed our morning slumbers indicated the state of the atmosphere; however, we entered Vopnafjord soon after mid-day, and shortly afterwards came to an anchorage opposite the town.

Vopnafjord is one of the homes of the eider duck,
and it was on the rocky islets opposite to the town
that we first saw those birds in their natural surroundings.   We borrowed one of the ship's boats and rowed
over to the rocks.   It was difficult to get near, for the
ducks were very shy—more so than usual just then,
because many had young; but as they were too
young to fly, we did get fairly near by rowing round
their rocks.   The nesting season was over, and many
of the birds had gone away.   The production of eider
down is an industry that is increasing; the birds are
rigorously protected, and a fine of ten kronur (eleven
shillings) is the penalty incurred by any one killing
an eider duck.

In the afternoon we went ashore in a hired boat
that leaked very badly; but we reached the shore
without anything very exciting happening.   The
return journey, however, was attended with considerable risk, for in the meantime the wind had
risen, and there was a nasty choppy sea beating
against us when we attempted to make the *Ceres.*
Water entered the boat through the leaky spots, and
more was shipped; we were near being swamped, but
we made the gangway, and got on board without anything worse than a wetting.   At the various ports of
call there was often considerable difficulty in obtain-
ing a boat, and the passenger wishing to get ashore
had to take whatever craft was available, for they
were very scarce.   Often they were dirty and very
leaky.   Sometimes a passage was refused, and on
one occasion a cargo-boat starting for the shore
declined a fare of two kronur, although going direct
to the wharf not far distant—the Icelander is an

independent personage, and unless it suits his convenience he sometimes refuses a job.

While at Vopnafjord we met with a man, an Icelander, who could speak a little English ; we soon discovered that he was proud of having acquired a few British swear words. Thomas and I were taking shots at a number of fish-cleaners at work on the beach, when this man came along ; we had previously been in conversation with him, so he remarked airily as he passed that the result of our snap would be " a hell of a picture." We laughed, but he went on a few paces and then stopped beside a fellow-passenger, a man of strict views and ideas, who was photographing the same subject. The Icelander, encouraged, I suppose, because we had laughed, went one better on what he had said to us, and gave his opinion that *this* result would be " a blank, blanketty blank picture " !—he seemed surprised at the freezingly cold way in which his remark was received.

We left Vopnafjord in the afternoon and in four hours made Langanes, a narrow, flat-topped peninsula several miles long, a perfectly horizontal lava flow, with faces that rise vertically from the sea ; the section is exactly the same, whether through the end or side of the peninsula. The whiteness of the points of rock and of the face generally, evidenced the fact that many sea-fowl resort there, and that the rock-face is covered with a deposit of guano.

At midnight we were inside the Arctic circle, and had the weather been favourable, we should have seen the sun just above the horizon. But His Majesty was not on view, for though the fog had lifted in the morning and had enabled us to make Vopnafjord,

the weather had been dull all day, with the sun quite
obscured, and the same conditions prevailed through
the night.   It was a pity, because it would probably
be our only chance of seeing the midnight sun, for
next day we should be in Akureyri, a town lying at
the head of a long fjord, and nearly a degree south
of the Arctic circle, where the view would, we thought,
be obscured by intervening hills and mountains.

Husavik in Skjalfandi was our next port of call,
and we arrived there early enough in the morning
for us to go ashore before breakfast.   Thomas and I
were interested in a reported "raised beach"—land
originally formed on the margin of the sea, and
subsequently raised by tectonic (subterranean) dis-
turbances to a height above sea-level.   Miss Hastie
was also desirous of seeing the raised beach, and
trudged along with us over the hills to the bay
where we expected to find it; but on arrival we
could see no raised beach : there was some volcanic
conglomerate, the rounded and smoothed stones of
which had perhaps caused it to be mistaken for a
raised beach—unless, indeed, we ourselves were on
the wrong track and had mistaken the spot; nevertheless, there was nothing else in view that looked
like what we were in search of, so we returned to
Husavik over the hills again.   Not long ago these
hills were completely covered with fine yellow
ferruginous loam—a comparatively recent deposit;
but it is now being rapidly eroded, and the older
moraine beneath laid bare.

At Husavik there is a great accumulation of
moraine matter that has been brought down from
the valley at the back.   It is a terminal moraine

that comes right down to the sea, which washes at the foot of its almost vertical face, fifty to sixty feet high. The town stands on the edge of the moraine, and the only approach from the pier is by a long flight of wooden steps; goods are conveyed in trucks that run up a steep inclined tramway, and these are raised and lowered by cables and the use of a windlass and friction brakes. Behind the town great fields of peat are being excavated and stacked ready for use as fuel.

On the voyage from Husavik to Akureyri, one of our fellow-passengers was the Icelandic minister of the church at Akureyri, a man who had a very fine tenor voice, the best in Iceland according to repute; at our request he sang to an accompaniment played on a small harp by a travelling companion. One thing he sang was the Icelandic National Hymn, entitled the "Hymn of Praise," composed by S. Sveinbjornsson to celebrate Iceland's thousand years of freedom. The thousand years were completed in 1874 (874 to 1874), and the fact was celebrated in that year with festivities and general rejoicing, the King of Denmark taking part in them.

On our arrival at Eyjafjord in the afternoon, the weather was clearing up, and as we steamed up the fjord fine views opened out, and we saw many excellent cloud-effects. After about three hours' steaming up the fjord we reached Akureyri, the town next in importance to Reykjavik, the capital, and came to an anchorage there at about eight o'clock in the evening.

CHAPTER IV

ACROSS THE NORTHERN INHABITED FRINGE

THE next day was a busy one with us, because Akureyri was to be our starting-point for the journey across the interior, and there were numerous preliminary arrangements to be made. The fogs and thick weather had delayed our arrival at Akureyri by a day. We ought to have set out from Akureyri on the day after our arrival, but the delay at sea had rendered that quite impossible, as may be imagined when I mention the facts that besides personal effects there were provisions, tents, bedding, etc., to be packed; that we were eleven persons in all (our own party of six, a conductor and manager of affairs, and four guides), and that thirty-eight ponies were required for our transport. Of course arrangements had been made for all this long before our leaving England.; ponies and everything else were there, but all required a lot of "licking into shape." Our manager was up to his eyes in it all day. The members of our party, however, had less to do, for when we had bought oilskins and sundries, and had sorted out and packed our personal effects into boxes specially made for the purpose—boxes that were to be carried on the ponies, one on each side of the pack-saddle—we were free to do as we liked for the rest of the day. It happened to be the anniversary of the Celebration of the Thousand Years of Freedom, and a festival was being held in Akureyri; so, on attaining *our* freedom, we made our way towards the fête ground, a spot named

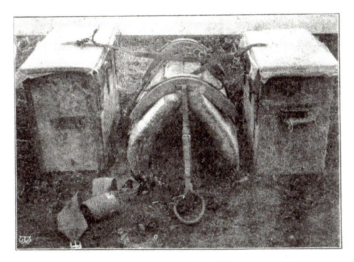

PACK-SADDLE AND BOXES.

Oddeyri, a sort of suburb about a mile away, on a spit of land running into the fjord. There we found the Icelanders assembled in force. People from all the surrounding country were there—men, women, and children; all had come on ponies, which were dotted about in groups, or straying separately over the spit—there were hundreds of them. The Icelanders were amusing themselves much as would the villagers at an English country fête. They were eating and drinking, and engaging in contests of various kinds. Races were being run, there were gymnastic competitions on "horse" and horizontal bar, and there was some wrestling also. The last was decidedly good and interesting. Each competitor grasped his opponent's right shoulder with left hand, and with the right took a firm hold of the other's waistband. Then the fun commenced. The opponents danced around each other, watching for opportunities. Their movements were very amusing, but some of the throws were very cleverly effected. In the evening, at about 8 P.M. that is, dancing commenced. A platform had been prepared for the purpose; this was railed round, and there were seats, on which the girls sat awaiting partners. The custom in choosing a partner is for the man to approach the lady of his choice and bow to her; she acquiesces by rising from her seat, when the couple waltz off together. Just before the dancing commenced, a good-humoured, rubicund man, short of stature, whose well-rounded figure denoted that he was not averse to the good things provided by the gods, ascended a rostrum at one end of the platform, and from there addressed the assemblage. To us who were not acquainted with the Icelandic tongue, his remarks were unintelligible; but by those around who were listening to his utterances, they seemed to be much appreciated, and their smiles and laughter showed that the orator, a fluent speaker, was a popular man and a humorist of no mean order; indeed, one had but to look at his expressive face when he was speaking to learn that he was a "funny" man.

Between the town of Akureyri and the basaltic

mountains to the westward that rise to a considerable altitude, there is, filling the interval, a series of morainic hills, the material of which has come down the Eyjafjorthará valley, or from the mountains beside it. These hills present the appearance of a terrace partly worn down and scored by the action of water and melting snow. No doubt

AKUREYRI AT MIDNIGHT.

the basaltic mountains once formed the side of the fjord. An hour or so before midnight, Miss Hastie, Thomas, and I climbed the hills to the terrace, in the hope of getting a glimpse of the midnight sun, for the night was almost cloudless. The sun was shining brightly, but it was quickly approaching some mountains near the entrance to Eyjafjord, behind which it would soon be hidden. We failed in the object of our climb, for the mountains referred

to were of considerable elevation. Time would not
allow us to attack the mountains in the rear of
Akureyri and ascend by midnight to an altitude
above that of the obscuring hills, so we had to
descend unsatisfied. Though we did not actually
see the *sun* at midnight, we could see its *light*
shining on the mountain tops two or three miles
away, and we knew that it was above the horizon.
So good was the light that Thomas and I took
photographs of the town, one looking north and
the other south, just at midnight—with stop *f*32,
exposures of one minute and one minute and a quarter
were required for medium plates.

We were to have made a start at eleven o'clock
the next morning, but fate was against us. At
the appointed hour the members of the party
were ready and waiting, but guides, ponies, pack
and riding saddles, tents, provisions, etc., were *not*
ready, and we could not well start unless they were.
Saddles and gear required many repairs—most of
them had been hired, and they were not in the best
condition. Our manager of affairs was to be seen
flitting about settling up accounts, giving directions to the men, inspecting saddles, bridles, girths,
and gear, and generally trying to reduce confusion
to order. For an hour or more we were amused,
but then we began to get impatient. Three of us
got hold of a saddle and bridle, and we tried the
paces of a few of the ponies. In that way we put
in an hour or two that might have proved irksome,
for everything was in such a state of confusion
and unreadiness, and the space in which the men
were working was so confined, that *we* could render

no effective help. Instead of starting at eleven, it was half-past three before we got away—four and a half hours late !

We made a slight stir as we clattered along the main street of the town, for it was the largest expedition of the kind that had ever set out from Akureyri, and the progress of our thirty-eight ponies

THE SPIT AT ODDEYRI.

was watched with some interest by those of the townspeople who were on the street. Our way lay beside the fjord, and we proceeded for several miles in a northerly direction. Our *general* direction across the island was, as a rule, southerly and westerly, but it was necessary to turn the end of a mountain chain before we could shape a more direct course. On we went, past Oddeyri, the scene of the previous day's festivities, until we reached

the Glerá, where we had our first experience of
fording an Icelandic river. It was not very deep,
and it was but a foretaste of a series of more difficult
fordings, not a few of which were serious under-
takings, and not to be attempted without proper con-
sideration. To this river, the Glerá, the formation
of the spit at Oddeyri is due. The detritus brought
down by its waters and deposited in the fjord has
been gradually banked up by the tides and storms
coming up Eyjafjord. Along the shores of the fjord
we passed over extensive ancient moraines; then by
a detour we worked round the edge of the moraines,
which form the end of the mountain range, and
entered Horgadalr (the valley of the Horgá). From
a spot where we had lunch, or whatever meal it
might be called—it was our first since breakfast—we
overlooked the valley of the Horgá. On the far side
there was a green, fertile-looking spot, and large
buildings, which we ascertained to be the Akureyri
agricultural grounds and college, presided over by
Professor Jon Hjaltalin. To the right the river ran
into the fjord through the valley, once, no doubt, an
indentation of Eyjafjord. At the mouth of the river
a small delta is in course of formation, which should
develop into a spit similar to that at Oddeyri.

Proceeding up the valley of the Horgá, many
interesting-looking peaks attracted our attention.
The valley and its branches having been eroded out
of basalt, the mountains and valleys are characteristic formations—pyramidal peaks, steep escarpments, deeply-cut gorges, with roaring torrents
rushing down in a series of waterfalls and broken
cascades; there are vast quantities of scree on the

mountain-sides covering the terraces of the lava
flows, and accumulations of similar material at the
foot of the mountains, forming a talus. Moraine
heaps are also numerous. Higher up the valley, just
above the confluence of the Horgá and the Oxnadalsá, there is a very striking scene, where the last-
named river has carved its way through a very

THE OXNADALSÁ CUTTING THROUGH A HARD DYKE.

hard dyke, the sides of which extend into the river,
and stand there like an immense wall with a gap
through it. While proceeding up Oxnadalr (the
valley of the Oxna = oxen), which is very picturesque,
we saw some fine cloud-effects as the moist air condensed and drifted just below the mountain tops.
The river Oxnadalsá takes its name from the valley,
Oxnadal. This is one of the few exceptions from
the general rule, which is for the valley to take its

name from the river—*dal* = valley; so, instead of Oxnadalsá, the rule would make it Oxná. Along this valley all the depressions in the hillsides are filled with quantities of peat. Peat, peat bogs, and swamps are very common throughout Iceland, and in most of the depressions in the hillsides and along the river valleys a peaty growth is to be found.

For several hours in the course of the day we were accompanied by a man travelling the same way and driving a pony laden with pieces of rather ancient shark. When travelling in company, the ponies have a way of crowding together, and unless very careful, one becomes painfully aware of the fact when box or bundle brushes in no gentle way against one's legs. Now the strange pony with the ancient shark at its sides was of a very friendly disposition, and evinced a desire to fraternise with our ponies, choosing the riding ponies for his special attentions, the result being that we had some difficulty in avoiding contact with the evil-smelling stuff. With this exception not many incidents worthy of special mention occurred on this our first day in the saddle; there were several breakdowns, however. The saddlery was not in the best possible condition; it was mostly old and weatherworn, and a great deal of it was very rotten. This became more apparent the farther we went: breakages were numerous, straps snapped, and packsaddles, bundles, and boxes broke away and were deposited by the wayside; while the ponies, glad to have got rid of their loads, careered gaily on. There was much bustle and confusion, rushing of guides (the men, whether acting as guides or not,

are all called guides) after the ponies. "Helvit!"
they would shout, as another strap broke and a
bundle trailed on the ground, bumping against lumps
of lava, by the pony's side; then they would urge
their steeds into a fast run or a canter, whistling
a soft, long-drawn-out note to induce the pony in
front to stop. To urge on the pony they utter a
shout that sounds like a cross between "haw" and
"hoch." "Hoch! hoch!" they shout, and sometimes bring their whips down with a swish upon
the haunches of the nearest pony. When they wish
a pony to stop or to slacken speed they whistle
gently. We soon found that it was useless to click
or to shout "Get up!" or "Wo!" to a pony. He
did not understand it, so we had to make use of the
sounds that they could recognise.

The first day's journey was not a very long one,
seven hours only in the saddle, and we reached our
first camping-ground at about half-past ten. Thverá
was the name of the farm-house beside which we
camped. The buildings were of very primitive construction; they were built in the usual Icelandic
style: turf walls and roof; wooden floors to the best
rooms, and earth or lava blocks to the others; glass
windows. The kitchen in most of the humbler class
of farm-houses is a picture, and this one was typical;
it was lighted only from the roof, and the openings
served also to ventilate the room and to act as smoke
shafts. A peat fire was burning in the corner of the
room, and the air was filled with the smoke that rose
from it and circulated round the room before escaping
through the openings in the roof. It had an earth
floor, and at the side of the room there was a well

about twenty feet deep, that supplied beautifully clear water for culinary purposes. A large cauldron stood over the fire, containing some savoury mess in course of preparation for the family's next meal.

We had four tents, two large ones and two smaller; but on this occasion we only made use of one of them, for four of our number slept at the farm-house. For the rest of the journey across Iceland, however, all four were in use. The two large ones were square "Bell" tents: one was used for meals, and in it the conductor and his four guides slept at night; in the other, Hill, Thomas, and I camped. Miss Hastie used one of the smaller tents; while the "nautical adviser" and the "handy man" occupied the other.

We did not make a start the next day till half-past one; it was several hours after that agreed upon, but we very soon learned that unpunctuality, delays in starting, and consequent waste of time would mark the journey; this was chiefly due to the rotten state of the gear, for several hours were spent every morning in patching up and tinkering at the packs, boxes, and saddles that had come to grief during the previous day—each day had its record of breakages and damage, and each morning its hours devoted to making repairs. All this was very annoying, and it made another guide almost a necessity to relieve one of the English-speaking guides, so that he might go on with us while the others were occupied with the repairs. This would have caused things to work better, but unfortunately no other guide was available. We were already on the edge of the fringe of population inhabiting the regions near the sea-coast, and we were fast approaching the uninhabited interior; there were no spare hands on the farms that we passed, so we were obliged to go on short-handed—short-handed *only* because of the continual breakages. The guides that we had could not have been improved upon: they were all first-class men, each was up to his work, and worked with a will; they were all Icelanders possessing small farms of

MORAINE ACCUMULATIONS AND CLOUD-EFFECTS AT THVERÁ.

their own, and two of them, Sigurthur and Hannes, spoke excellent English; Thorlakur was a beginner at it, but we generally managed to understand one another; the fourth man, Josef, was the only one who had no knowledge of our language. We were on excellent terms with all the guides, so things worked smoothly between us.

On leaving Thverá our way, as we ascended some three or four hundred feet to the head of the valley, lay at first over a vast accumulation of moraine matter, piled high up on all sides. Our camping ground had been at the foot of this accumulation, and opposite to it on the other side of the valley there were also great heaps of similar stuff, while on the highest part of the range there was a very fine pinnacle rock, rising several hundred feet higher, and standing out sharp against the clear sky.

I had a bad day of it, being quite out of luck. The conductor accidentally backed his pony upon me, and my right foot was crushed and bruised beneath one of its hoofs; but worse was to come. About an hour after we had started, and when we were getting well up into the moraine, I heard a shout. " Helvit! Helvit!" cried one of the guides. On looking ahead I saw a pony running amuck through the rough broken lava and great boulders; he had got rid of most of his load, but something green was trailing at his heels. In horror I watched the pony's wild career, for the "something green" I recognised as the cover of my plane-table—one of the instruments that I had brought for the purpose of mapping a portion of the interior. This plane-table had been strapped on the top of some packs containing bedding, in order that it might ride on something soft and in safety. I comprehended what had happened. As usual something had given way, the packs and my plane-table had got loose about the pony's heels, and all had been kicked off *except* the plane-table, which had been made fast by one of its straps to a ring in the pack-saddle, and as the strap was sound it had held on. Well, there was no mistaking its Willesden canvas cover—there it was, trailing along

at the pony's heels, being kicked and banged against
boulders great and small, just as they came in the
way. Bumpity-thump it went along the ground,
and with a crash it struck the boulders! The table
was ruined, for it trailed a mere crumpled mass without definite shape. There was an end to prospects
of mapping. I watched the pony's career for a
moment, more in sorrow than in anger, then I urged
my own pony into a canter, and came up with the
runaway just as one of the guides caught him. The
wreck of the plane-table was soon detached from the
pack-saddle; a hasty inspection proved that my fears
were confirmed: the table itself was represented by
a couple of strips, the rest of it was missing; the
tripod stand and the alidade ruler were also missing.
The guides scoured the neighbourhood of the pony's
course, and after a while one of them turned up with
one or two strips of wood, pieces of the plane-table,
and placed them beside the others. I looked on
listlessly until another guide brought in a long green
case. This did not seem to be much damaged, so
I hastily examined the contents (the tripod stand
and the ruler), and found to my joy that they were
practically uninjured; a few bruises to the legs did
not matter much, for they did not affect the stability
of the stand—both alidade and stand could be used!
I then turned to the wreck of the table itself and
examined the pieces; they were not complete, two or
three were missing, but I noticed that although all
the screws had been wrenched out, and the apparatus
for fixing the board to the stand had also been
wrenched off, yet the breaks and splinters were all
along the grain of the wood. The guides went over

the ground again, and brought back one or two
additional strips. I then roughly put the pieces
together, and found that except for a few splinters
I had got them all, and that *none* was broken *across*
the grain ; the two cross-bars for the back, the last
pieces found, were also unbroken. It looked as if it
might be roughly mended, *if* only the necessary tools
were available.

THE WRECKÉD PLANE-TABLE.

The views in the valley of the Oxnadalsá were
fine, and the river scenery where the water had
carved deep down through the lava and tuff was
very bold, the red and blue tints of a quantity of
scoria on the steep banks adding to the effect.

In the evening we crossed the water-parting, or
divide, between the Oxnadalsá and the Northrá
rivers, and at night camped beside a farm known
as Fremrikot near the head of the valley of the

Northrá river (Northradal). It was a picturesque spot, and the Northrá is typical of the smaller rivers of the country, the valley filled with alluvium and the river meandering through it, though when in flood not much of the alluvium can be seen.

In the morning I amused myself by taking photographs. I caught the women and children from the

THE NORTHRÁ.

farm sitting with their backs against an earth-built fence looking with interest at, and discussing, the preparations then being made for a start; these preparations are shown in the view looking down the valley of the Northrá where saddling up is nearly completed.

We received a check this day, and made very little progress. We started gaily enough and fairly early, as times went with us—that is, we got away a

quarter of an hour after mid-day—and pursued our
way along Northradal.   There were several fine
gorges with torrents coming down from the mountains into the Northrá; one especially attracted us,
where a big snow-water torrent rushes between great
buttresses of rock standing on each side.   There is
a bridge across the gorge, for the torrent is quite
unfordable.   After about two hours' riding down the

SADDLING UP.

valley of the Northrá to its confluence with the
Herradsvötn we soon reached Silfrastathr, where, in
a picturesque spot, there are a farm-house and a small
octagonal church.   Here we lunched and made a
long halt while the guides went on to ascertain
whether the Herradsvötn, one of the big rivers of
the journey, was fordable.   It was past five when
they returned with a local guide and the news that
it could not then be forded, because the water from

that day's melted snow was coming down and the
river too much swollen.   On a warm day the snow
in the mountains melts rapidly, and a large increase
in the volume of the water results ; so that there is
much more coming down in the afternoon than in
the early morning before the sun's heat causes the
snow to melt.

Farther on, when describing one of the quicksand
rivers that we crossed, I refer to the dangerous nature
of their passage ; but I find it necessary to make
special mention of the subject here, for while revis-
ing these notes, bad news reached me concerning the
Herradsvötn.   In July last year an accident happened
at this river which resulted in the death of our
"conductor" of the previous year.   We did not
regard the Herradsvötn as a quicksand river, but it
seems to be one, for the account of the accident states
that our conductor's horse got into a quicksand and
threw his rider, who was carried down the river so
quickly by the swift current that no assistance could
be rendered, and he was drowned, his body not being
recovered until two days afterwards.   Poor fellow,
his first crossing with us was accomplished safely,
and I little thought that I should have to record
his death as the result of the second attempt.   I
happened to take two photographs of this river, one
having Maelifellshnukr in the background, and showing the many streams into which the river is split
up, the other showing the members of our party
about to cross the first stream.   Fourteen of the
ponies can be seen in the latter, but the great
majority of the pack-ponies were ahead, out of the
picture—it was impossible to get a string of thirty-

eight ponies into one quarter-plate view; the conductor leads our party, and is the first following the tail of the pack-train, he with right hand behind back. The danger in these quicksand rivers is due to the fact that the sands are continually shifting; in the summer each day has its flood of snow water which scours the bed of the river, removing the sand from one

CROSSING THE HERRADSVÖTN.

place and depositing it in another, so that one definite course cannot always be followed when crossing; what is a good ford one day is impassable the next. With a river split up into about twenty streams the difficulties of fording can be imagined, but not appreciated until experienced, and the dread with which all the guides regard the rivers where quicksands are known to exist cannot be wondered at.

As the river was not fordable, there was nothing

for us to do but await the falling of the water, and then attempt the passage. The delay enabled me to try my hand at repairing the plane-table. The "handy man" was useful on this occasion, as on many others, for he produced from his capacious pockets a wonderful knife. Now this knife had a screw-driver blade that enabled me to countersink a number of holes in the cross pieces, thus permitting the short screws to "bite" in sound places in the broken pieces of the table. In a couple of hours we emerged triumphantly from a room in the farm-house that we had "commandeered" as a workshop, with the patched-up wreck bearing some semblance to a plane-table; it was certainly not in any way perfect, but it looked as if it might with care be used.

In the afternoon I was about to take a photograph of the farm-house; there were several girls standing in front of it, who, when they saw me point my camera, at once took to their heels and ran away (much to my surprise), laughing merrily as they disappeared through an open doorway. Thereafter when they saw me camera in hand they always bolted for the house; this made me determine to have a photograph of them; so I lay in wait, and when next they were running away, I took a snap as they were making straight for the doorway; the photograph, however, was a failure.

Maelifellshnukr, a prominent feature in the landscape here, is a mountain between three and four thousand feet high: it is prominent not only from Silfrastathr, but it can be seen from many places within a radius of sixty or seventy miles, and I afterwards saw it from several widely separated spots.

The pronunciation of some of the Icelandic words is rather puzzling to a new-comer; for instance, the first part of the name of this mountain is pronounced as if spelt may-lee-fettle—*tl* instead of double *l*.

The churches in Iceland are often put to strange uses (strange to foreigners, that is); many are the property of the farmers on whose land and beside whose houses they are built. A clergyman often has three or four of these farmers' churches in his district, and he holds occasional services in them. It is a custom, when the farm-house has not proper guest-chambers, for travellers to sleep in the church, and *we* did so in that at Silfrastathr, Miss Hastie using her own tent as usual. Our beds were arranged some on the floor and others suspended between the seats. The following photograph of the interior of the church taken at midnight shows some of our party peacefully slumbering in their beds.

Next day we made an early start, for we got away soon aften ten o'clock, in order to ford the river before the melting snow caused the waters to rise. There was a considerable difference in the level, for I found on going down for my tub that a small branch in which I had the previous afternoon tested the temperature of the water was non-existent. This temperature-testing had caused some fun, for in using my sling thermometer for the purpose, I tied it to the end of my riding-whip, and thus held it suspended in the stream. Hill, catching me in the act, made a sketch which he entitled: "Our lunatic fishing with his thermometer as bait," and handed it round at our evening meal.

The report of the local guide as to the state of

the river was a favourable one, so we proceeded down
to the Herradsvötn, and prepared against probable
wettings. Each had his own fancy for keeping out
the water. Miss Hastie wore india-rubber top-boots
—I have omitted to say that she rode astride, by far
the best way for the rough work in Iceland; the
"nautical adviser" used waterproof leggings, the

SILFRASTATHR CHURCH. ASLEEP AT MIDNIGHT.

"handy man" top-boots, Hill sheepskin top-boots
of native manufacture, Thomas did not seem to care
whether he got wet or not, while I put on india-
rubber shoes and chanced the rest. There were some
interesting and picturesque costumes in the group.

When all was ready, the local guide led off with
some of the pack, three of our own guides following
with other sections of it; the conductor went next,
and the members of our party followed; I stayed

behind for a few minutes to photograph the crossing of the first branch of the river, and then brought up the rear with the other guide. The river runs over a very broad bed and is divided into something like twenty streams, so a considerable time—about half an hour—was occupied before the last stream had been forded. The water was rather deep in some of the branches, and came up just to our knees. We made a very satisfactory crossing, and reached the other side without incident worth recording; a few hours later it would have been impassable again. The river was no doubt " up " when our conductor lost his life.

While crossing the river there was a very distinct mirage effect when looking down it towards the sea. Some of us took shots with cameras, but nothing resulted; it was too distant.

Two days before, and again during this day, there were breakages innumerable; the state of the pack-saddles, packs, straps, girths, bridles, etc., was simply disgraceful—there is no other word for it! Several falls had been due to the breaking of reins or girths, and by the end of the day there was scarcely a member of the party who had not come to grief in this way. Thomas, who was riding a spirited beast, came two croppers through his reins breaking: the second time his pony rolled upon him and he strained a muscle in his side; this was unfortunate, for he felt the effects more or less to the end of the journey. From the river valley, where Thomas had one fall, we ascended to the top of Tungusveit, a long narrow ridge that extends for about twenty miles, dividing the Herradsvötn and Svartá rivers. These long ridges, with rivers flowing in parallel lines on each side, form one of the geographical features of Iceland. Many of them are to be seen in different parts of the country. From this ridge, on which there were many "erratic" boulders, a fine view of Maelifell-shnukr was obtained; at the foot of the peak beyond the Svartá there is a series of morainic hills.

At Maelifell below the mountain there is a parsonage and farm-house, where we halted for a light luncheon. At these farm-houses milk and coffee can always be obtained, and sometimes excellent home-made biscuits and cake also, and these delicacies were forthcoming here. The Icelanders are noted for the good quality of their coffee, which may be regarded as the national drink.

Up to this point we had followed the more or less beaten tracks pursued by farmers and others in travelling from farm to farm; but we were now on the extreme edge of the fringe of population, and were about to plunge into the uninhabited interior. We decided to attack a route that had been used years before by the settlers and farmers—when the present good and frequent service of coasting steamers was not running—to convey fish, other provisions, etc., from and to the coast and across the island, and we found it a very interesting one. ·

We proceeded up the valley of the Svartá for a few miles over accumulations of river deposits, till we reached Ġilhagi farm-house, where we halted for our mid-day meal. This was the last house met with on the north side of the desert and ice-bound interior, and we did not again see signs of habitation till arriving within two days of Reykjavik.

Mention must be made of an amusing misunderstanding that had occurred on the score of matches.
It seems that the "nautical adviser" before leaving
Akureyri had inquired of the conductor whether he
had plenty of matches, and the latter had replied
that he had plenty—and so he had for the ordinary
requirements of the camp, but not for the general
use of smokers; the conductor in his reply had
thought only of the camp, while the other had asked
from a smoker's point of view, hence there was an
approach to a famine as regards the smokers, and it
was pathetic sometimes to see the "nautical adviser"
and the "handy man" carefully husbanding a match,
in the hope that the supply would hold out to Reykjavik.

At Gilhagi the women were washing wool; there
was a fire in the open beside a small stream of water,
and on the fire a cauldron, in which the wool was
boiled; it was afterwards washed in the running
water.

CHAPTER V

WE were delayed for about two hours while waiting for the farmer to conduct us over the mountains ; it was necessary to take a local guide, for none of our own men had ever been over the ground. When we did move on we tried to make up in pace for the delay ; we made good time in ascending steadily from the valley over great accumulations of moraine matter and by ancient tracks through hummocky land. Riding through this hummocky ground some- times requires the exercise of considerable caution. The continuous traffic of generations across the hummocks wore innumerable tracks, which have since been kept open by the weather, and deepened in some cases. Many of them are very deep, occa- sionally reaching almost to the knees. One has to raise first one foot and then the other to prevent their being badly crushed, or to avoid being unhorsed by contact with the sides as the ponies go on at a fast jog-trot. One member of the party caught both feet against the sides of the ruts, with the result that he was thrown forward, when he affectionately clasped his pony round the neck.

51

As we continued to ascend we met with a new experience, for we had to ride up one fairly long snow slope and several smaller ones, following in the tracks of the pack-train over the beaten-down snow. We were then at a considerable altitude, perhaps 2500 feet, and we entered what is known as Litli-sandr, the little sand waste. Its name does not quite describe it—waste it is, and desolate enough,

CROSSING A SMALL SNOW SLOPE.

but there is not a great deal of sand in the part that we traversed, and we passed through its middle. It is an elevated moraine, comparatively flat, with a number of small lakes whose existence is due to a series of drift dams. It was very cold while we were crossing Litlisandr, for the icy wind was blowing strongly in our faces, so the latter part of the day's journey—a long one, for we did not reach camp till just a quarter of an hour before midnight—was made under considerable personal discomfort.

The going was very rough, and some very steep

slopes had to be descended after crossing the *sandr*, and nothing but the sure-footed ponies of Iceland could have got down them in safety. These ponies are hardy little beasts, averaging about twelve hands; born and bred in the hills, they are accustomed to forage for a living in the roughest country, and their experiences there cause them to become the sure-footed beasts that they are. They seem to run on three legs, for they always have a spare one ready for emergencies. Some of them stumble badly, but as a rule they do not, and it is a very rare thing for a pony to come down. It is wonderful how hard they keep on nothing but green feed; they never see a bit of " hard tack," yet, when required, they can jog along for twelve hours or more and be fresh at the end.

After descending from the *sandr*, we traversed more moraine matter until we reached our camping-ground at Athalmansvötn. Here there are two lakes, and it was on the banks of the more northerly Athalmansvatn that we camped. At the end of our journeys, especially when arriving late, as we did on this occasion, our hands and feet were icily cold—so cold that, to induce a better circulation, we were wont to seize mallets and drive in tent pegs, or to do something else requiring vigorous muscular exertion.

On our way over the *sandr* we saw the most magnificent sunset effects. Indeed, it was often our luck to witness the glories of an Icelandic sunset.

Towards morning a gale of wind struck us, and threatened to blow our tents into the lake. Fortunately the tents and their cords were sound, and

the pegs driven well into the ground, so we escaped
the discomfort of a sudden exposure to wind and
weather.

Next day we reverted to the usual habit of
starting late; but on this occasion it was excusable,
for our dinner, or supper, or whatever name may be
applied to our third meal, was not finished till past
1 A.M., so a start at 1 P.M. was not so late as it
appeared. As it was difficult to draw a line between
day and night, an hour or two one way or the other
did not matter very much.

Some of our party had hurts which they nursed
tenderly: the "nautical adviser" had a knee,
Thomas a side, and so on; and great was the con-
sumption of "Elliman's" and "Homocea," advantage
being taken of the halts to rub in one or other of
these remedies for ills of all kinds; but the "nautical
adviser" and Thomas did not seem to take much
heed of their hurts when they were in the saddle, for
they rode hard enough over the rough moraines that
we crossed. At first our course lay over soft peaty
ground, but afterwards we were obliged to pick our
way over expanses of great boulders. We had to
ascend for a while, but suddenly, from the ridge at
the highest point in our ascent, there was opened to
us a fine panoramic view of two of Iceland's great
ice-fields, Hoff Jökull and Lang Jökull. A number
of prominent peaks stood out boldly, chief among
them being Hrutafell, Skeljafiall, Kjalfell, and those
of Kerlingarfjöll.

Our next experience was in crossing a wind-blown
sand desert, where the wind blew the sand in clouds
across our path and we had ocular demonstration of

the work performed in such regions by the wind, where great clouds of sand sweep onward day after day, encroaching upon the land and continually altering the surface features. Although this is a genuine *sandr* it is not so marked on the maps. We covered several miles before we got clear of this sand-blown desert and entered a region of ordinary moraine matter.

After lunching beside a small brook we continued over the moraine to the river Strangákvisl. The pack had gone on ahead while we were at lunch, but one guide was left behind to pilot us across the river, which is noted for the number of quicksands in its bed. There is a considerable spice of danger in crossing these quicksand rivers, for a pony sometimes gets into the soft treacherous bottom, and the rider runs the risk of a ducking, even if nothing more serious happens. The guides have a wholesome dread of the rivers where quicksands are known to exist, and not without due cause. No definite and fixed course can be taken—the quicksands are always changing their positions. The guide went first, as usual, and we were preparing to follow, when suddenly we saw his pony falter and then plunge wildly as he sank into soft sand. The guide was about to jump into the water in order to relieve the pony, and to distribute the weight over a greater area—this is always done as soon as the nature of the bottom is ascertained—when the pony struggled upon a hard bottom and righted himself. Another course was then chosen, and we all got over without finding any quicksand.

A succession of moraines brought us to the banks of a broad river, the Blandá, having several channels and a reputation for quicksands. By this time we had caught up the pack-train, but we waited while it crossed the river, one guide staying behind to pilot us after the pack had safely accomplished the crossing. The guide marked with big stones the point of entrance and then watched intently—as did we all —the passage of the river by the pack. It was forded, however, without misadventure, so we followed carefully in the track pursued by the train. The conductor's pony slipped in the middle of the river and nearly threw his rider into the water, but a quick recovery by the pony prevented a disagreeable wetting and an uncomfortable ride. We had a third river to cross before the day's fording was over. A quantity of moraine and hummocky land intervened, but that was traversed without incident worth recording. The third river is a second Blandá, a branch of the other Blandá; it is really the main river whose proper name is the Beljandi, but the people do not recognise that name, or so speak of it. Although not a quicksand river, most members of the party narrowly escaped coming to grief. It was very deep at the start, and there were some deeper holes not far from the bank; it had to be entered at a very sharp angle, and with a bit of a drop close to the steep bank. Miss Hastie was the first nearly to come to grief: her pony suddenly dived into one of the deep holes, and she herself was taking a header when her pony made a wonderful recovery from its plunge into the hole, and set her straight again; she, however, was unfortunate in straining her side, but she afterwards pluckily kept on the way; all the others following, with one exception, got into one or another of the deep holes ; but they all escaped complete submersion, though wetted about legs and feet. I was the exception, for I was riding last—a position that enabled me to profit by the misfortunes of the others and avoid all the holes. I had a way frequently of bringing up the rear, because of stoppages made to take passing shots with camera at things of interest. This camera was always strapped to one of the rings of my saddle, where, on a comfortable pad on the off-side, it rode in safety—except when I happened to bring my whip down heavily upon it instead of upon the pony. The result of these stoppages was, that there was sometimes a delay in the crossing of a river, or a wait at an awkward spot, or at a point of divergence. It often happened that in coming up with the main party, I found my companions shivering from the effects of inaction in a cold wind —the wind *is* cold when it blows from one of the ice-fields—and in a frame of mind that must have been affected by the wind, judging from the freezingly cold manner in which I was received.

After crossing the river, we continued along near to its banks for several miles. In a pool just below some small rapids, the only rapids we had seen, there were several swans. Our course lay, as usual, over moraine matter and hummocky land, but there was a big patch of black sand composed of fine lava particles that we had to cross. Thus we proceeded until reaching Hveravellir, our next camping-ground, where we found a complete change in the appearance of the country.

We seemed to have got clear of hummocks and boulders, and to have reached the margin of fairyland, for we found ourselves, with grass around, looking at a series of hot springs, fumaroles, and sinter terraces, down which azure blue water trickled, lodging in a number of basins in the terraces, and adding by its colour to the beauty of the scene. Visions of the delights of a natural warm bath rose before me as I looked upon the terraces, recalling the luxury of bathing at the Pink Terraces in New Zealand, before their destruction by the eruption of Mount Tarawera. There are many pleasures in anticipation, for we did not enjoy warm bathing here; we had none; the water was too hot and the basins too small—though there was one small pot-hole in which the water was not very hot, where one could, with the aid of a big sponge, imagine better things, for the water did not look clean and sparkling and blue as in other basins.

Miss Hastie might have had an awkward experience at the spring where she elected to perform her ablutions, of whose periodical activity she was at the time unaware. During breakfast, one of the guides informed us that the small geyser Miss Hastie had been using as her hot-water tap had "gone off." Subsequent experience proved such pools untrustworthy for washing of any kind. A number of handkerchiefs left by themselves to soak were found an hour or two later making their way down an escape hole in the basin, and one that had been entirely absorbed by suction was *not* returned during a subsequent eruption by the dishonest geyser.

We erected our tents beside a blue warm-water stream facing the sinter terraces, and as the next day was Sunday, we camped there for two nights.

We all took a number of photographs of the terraces and the hot springs, and tried to catch the small geysers when they erupted, as with a few exceptions they did at short intervals; it is true that the eruption was not very violent, and the water was not thrown to a great height, three feet, perhaps, being the maximum.

HVERAVELLIR—THE SINTER TERRACES.

The next day was devoted to exploring the surrounding neighbourhood, and the different members of the party were struck with different features. Thomas and I set off together. We made for the higher ground, and looked round; we at once saw that we were at the edge of a recent (geologically) lava flow. About four miles distant there stuck up two horns, which we afterwards discovered to be the only prominent remains of the cone of the

volcano, Strytur, whence the lava had been ejected.
Strytur stands in the middle of the long strip of
country lying between, and about equidistant from,
the two great ice-fields, Lang Jökull and Hoff Jökull,
the area of each of which is roughly about five hundred
square miles. The strip is about *fourteen* miles wide
at its narrowest part (not eight as shown on the
existing maps), and extends north and south about
twenty-five miles. Strytur is on the divide, or water-
parting, between one system of rivers flowing north
and another flowing south, and it stands on the highest
part of this strip of land. The lava, as it issued from
the volcano, flowed north and south down gentle
declivities, and spread out east and west almost
to the outlying ranges on the margins of the ice-
fields. North it extends to just beyond Dufufell,
and south almost to Lake Hvitarvatn. I had come
to this part of the country intending to make a
quick survey of it as we traversed it from end to
end; Thomas also wished to note its structure, so
we both looked with interest over the expanse of
broken lava spread out before us. It was the
roughest possible country to survey (as was subsequently proved), and we were not altogether taken
with the task before us. We made our way to a
prominent peak of lava that rose forty or fifty feet
above the general level, and thence looked around.
I wanted a line on which to base my survey, and
I decided that this peak and a similar peak, lying in
an easterly direction about a mile away, would be
suitable elevated ends for a base line.

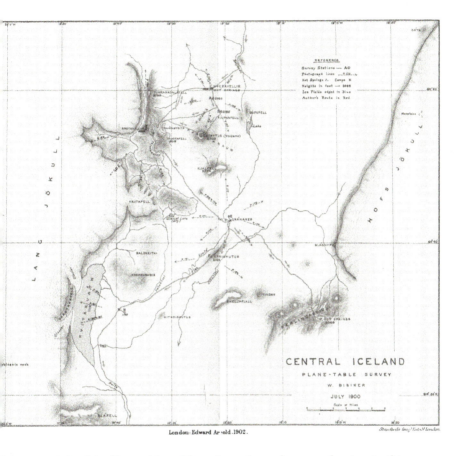

CENTRAL ICELAND

PLANE-TABLE SURVEY

W. BISIKER

JULY 1900

Scale of Miles

London: Edward Arnold. 1902.

The material originally positioned here is too large for reproduction in this reissue. A PDF can be downloaded from the web address given on page iv of this book, by clicking on 'Resources Available'.

CHAPTER VI

THE INTERIOR—STRYTUR AND ITS LAVA

I COMMENCED my survey the next morning before breakfast, when I went out to the first position on the lava-peaks and there set up the plane-table, that table which had so badly come to grief at the heels of the runaway pony a few days before. My drawing-paper had been kicked to pieces and was quite useless, and it was only by a chance that I was able to attempt a survey at all. At Edinburgh, just before starting, Thomas bought two or three small sheets of drawing-paper for his own work, in order to be independent of my supply; it was lucky that he had done so, for I was thus able to borrow from him. The size of the sheets was much smaller than mine, and they did not nearly fill the table; it did not much matter though, for part of the table was quite unfit to work upon, because of the long holes where splinters were missing; of course, the area of country capable of being mapped on a sheet was reduced according to the size, and it meant the use of a greater number of sheets of paper, which was a disadvantage; but the board of the plane-table *could* with care be worked upon, and there *was* paper avail-

able.   Having set up the plane-table in position, I
erected a flag-post and returned to camp to breakfast.
I found that Thomas had, in the meantime, made a
small survey on his own account of a line of fissure
running through the hot springs of Hveravellir, and
had located the position of the springs on that line.

The morning was so beautifully fine, and the sun
shining so brightly, that we breakfasted in the open
at tables erected in front of the tents.   We photographed the camp and the party, with the guides at
ease close by.   The frontispiece is from a negative,
the property of Miss Hastie, which was taken by the
conductor.   Our meals were not always taken under
such favourable conditions—the weather, as a rule, was
not good enough.   We generally had them under cover
of a tent, where we messed in much closer quarters,
small accidents being not uncommon in consequence.
One morning they were more numerous than usual :
the soup took a long time to boil, and when at last
it was hot enough, the conductor stumbled and spilled
some of the precious liquid over the " handy man,"
who would have preferred an internal application ;
then somebody upset the coffee ; soon afterwards
ominous creaks were heard to proceed from where
the " nautical adviser " was seated on his camp-stool,
which finally collapsed, and our heavy-weight measured
his length on the ground.   But such incidents as these,
trivial as they were, served to enliven us ; they were
specially diverting when the weather was adverse.

The weather gave promise of great things, so
Thomas and I started away for our first position full
of good intentions.   I soon got to work, and made
excellent progress with my plane-tabling ; but gradually

there was a change, the sky clouded over, and before long rain began to fall; now, to work at a plane-table in the rain is impossible, so I had to stop. We decided instead to measure along our base line towards the second position at the other end of it. We started in a drizzling rain, which increased as we proceeded; it was very difficult work, for the line was over the roughest possible lava-field. We made good progress, however, but when we had measured thirteen-sixteenths of a mile, it was raining so heavily that, wet through as we then were, and with boots filled with water, we resolved to abandon work for the day. After we had started in the morning, the rest of the party proceeded to the next camping-ground, a few miles farther on, at Thjofadal—a valley at the foot of the big mountain of the region, Hruta-fell. For this camp we made tracks over a perfect wilderness, where the fantastic shapes assumed by the lava were most wonderful. There were vents innumerable, including a number of the fissure type; arches, too, that had resulted from side pressure; also many other peculiar forms : pillars, circular vents, etc. On nearing Thjofadal we emerged from the lava and entered upon the moraines at the foot of the range bordering the great ice-field of Lang Jökull. Passing over one of the spurs running down from this outlying range, we dropped by a steep descent into the valley of the Thjofadalsá, a small stream on the south side of the ridge known as Kjalhraun (lava ridge) that crosses the lava-field by way of Strytur, the highest spot in it.

The next morning Thomas and I returned to our first position. Originally most of us had intended to make an attack upon Hrutafell, the giant peak of Lang Jökull; but the rain had delayed my work by the greater part of a day, so Thomas and I had to give up all idea of attempting the ascent. The idea was finally abandoned by the other members of the party, but a preliminary survey of the difficulties was made by the conductor, who thought that he could see a way that might render a successful ascent possible. The " handy man," being released from the Hrutafell expedition, offered to lend a hand in measuring the remainder of the base line, so he accompanied us back to position number one; we also took Thorlakur, one of the guides, with us. On the way, which was along the foot of the range outlying Lang Jökull, we had to pass over a small snow-field, close to which we came upon a good specimen of ropy lava.

After taking several photographs from my first position, we proceeded along the base line to where a staff had been left to mark the point already reached, and thence continued our measurements to the second position at the other end of the base. We found the two positions to be nearly a mile and a quarter apart. A more difficult piece of measurement could not be imagined, taken as the line was over the extremely rough surface of a broken-up scoriaceous lava-field. We remained at the peak forming the second end of the base line for several hours, during which period I was very busy at the plane-table. We then proceeded towards the volcano, Strytur, across the lava, and found it a scene of the wildest and most fantastic desolation—a constant succession of rough lava, ropy surfaces, vents, arches, snow-fields, and small lakes of icy coldness formed by melting snow. Occasion-

ally we had an unpleasant variation, for there were
many bogs that appeared to be quite solid until the
plunging of a pony, as it sank into one of them,
told us that the apparently hard-looking surface was
a mass of mud with a number of lava blocks and
stones set in it.

Arrived at Strytur, another indescribable scene of
desolation met our view. The lava was twisted and
contorted in the wildest manner, and mixed in the
utmost confusion. The volcano has two craters, inner
and outer ; the former rather more than three-eighths
of a mile, and the latter nearly five-eighths in
diameter. The two horns are of peculiar shape : the
western horn being but an isolated pinnacle rising
less than a hundred feet above its surroundings ; the
eastern horn is another isolated peak, but though one
side of it is perpendicular, and goes deep down into
the inner crater, the other side falls gradually away
in the typical slope of a volcano. These two horns
stand up as distinct landmarks, and can be seen from
a great distance to the north ; in the south, however,
they are hidden, by intervening hills and mountains,
from many places that are but a short distance away.
The inner crater contains much lava debris, some of
the blocks being of enormous size, while in several
places there is snow of unknown depth.

My third position was on the highest point of the
eastern horn. The wind was very cold, blowing as
it was direct from the ice-field, and my companions
who had but little work to do had a trying time of it
in such an exposed position. They stood shivering
in the cold, but descended after a while to the foot
of the horn, whence they whistled away at short

F

intervals in an endeavour to hurry me over the
work; but as there was no rain, I had, in spite of
cold winds, to stick to it, and take advantage of the
opportunity to work at the plane-table. I was hailed
with delight when I did descend — delight at the
prospect of getting away from such a bleak, inhospitable spot. The view from Strytur looking towards
Hrutafell and the ice and snow field of Lang Jökull
is very fine. Once more we crossed the lava-field
and made the best of the way to our camp at
Thjofadal.

Next day I was obliged to go on with my work
without a companion, and had not a smooth time of
it altogether; things did not go right. Over-night
I had determined to fix my fourth position on the
mountain Rauthkollur, the highest point at the
southern end of the outlying range of Lang Jökull.
I set out alone, for Thomas was in trouble with his
side, and the "handy man" did not look upon the
expedition with much interest, for the weather was
most unfavourable for any one not having special
work to do—rain, hail, snow, and blow were the
conditions that held during the whole of the time
that I was away from camp. The way lay up a steep
gorge between the mountain and a spur running
down from near the end of the range; the slopes of
the gorge were covered with scree that gave way at
every step, and often I slid back several yards before
I could stop myself. The climb was a stiff and very
uncomfortable one, laden as I was with instruments,
glasses, camera, and plane-table; but by sticking to
it I gradually ascended yard by yard. I got off the
scree whenever possible, and climbed up the course

of a small mountain stream; but there were many
waterfalls that could not be climbed, which caused
me to return to the scree again and again, often
sending the loose material flying down in a series
of landslips. Higher up I skirted several small snow-
fields, where better progress was possible, for the scree
at the edges of the snow did not slip away so freely.
The ascent would have been easy enough had I not
been so heavily and awkwardly laden, or had my
hands been free.

At the summit of Rauthkollur a glorious view
rewarded me. In front stretched the great ice-field
of Lang Jökull; away to the left was the giant
Hrutafell: three of its glaciers faced me, while a
fourth could just be seen at right angles to the
others. The back of this mountain merges in a
series of hills that are set in the ice of Lang Jökull.
Below Hrutafell, and at the foot of the ice-cap of
Lang Jökull, a perfect network of streams came
from the snow and ice; it was interesting to trace
their meanderings as they ran into stream after
stream, until finally all joined in one swift-running
torrent and flowed at the foot of the moraines below
Hrutafell. Away to the right I looked along the
outlying range, on the end peak of which I was
standing, and down into the valley between the
range and the ice-field.

In spite of the adverse weather, my plane-tabling
was very successful from this station; its command-
ing position enabled me to obtain a good view of the
surrounding country, not only over the ice-field, but
also over the country from which the ascent had
been made. I looked down into Thjofadal, right

over the mountain Thjofafell, across the lava-field to
Strytur and Kjalfell, and to the ice-field of Hoff
Jökull beyond. Showers had to be dodged and
plane-tabling done when it did not rain or snow;
but I filled up the intervals by taking several
photographs, and by making a boiling-point observation for altitude, also clinometer observations for
calculating the heights of surrounding peaks.

The return to camp was made at a quicker rate
than the ascent; but I met with a nasty accident, by
slipping on a stone in the gorge and diving head
first down a small waterfall into a pool of water
below. The plane-table turned over, and coming
upon me, pinned me down in the water for a
few seconds; the camera was underneath in the
water, which was flowing through it, for the outside
case was not water-tight. I extricated myself in
course of time, not much the worse for the fall; a
badly bruised knee, the loss of a quantity of skin
from hands, and a few minor bruises, being all
the damage that I had received—it might have
been much worse, laden as I was. On arrival in
camp I was patched up, and the "nautical adviser"
busied himself in preparing soup and other comforts for the inner man, for which attentions I was
grateful.

The other members of the party had not done
very much in the bad weather, one or two small
excursions to spots in the neighbourhood excepted.
Late in the afternoon we struck camp and moved on
a few miles farther, to a spot known as Gránanes,
right on the other side of the lava-fields. Our way
lay round by Hrutafell by the side of the river

Falakvisl, which runs in a deep gorge at the foot
of the mountain.   From this river we struck across
rough lava, then moraine matter, and again lava
right up to the river Svatá.   The rivers, as a rule,
run along at the edges of the lava flows ; there are
some exceptions, however, and one instance, in the
west of the island, I will refer to in its proper place.

A VOLCANIC VENT OF THE FISSURE TYPE.

One very fine vent we came upon when crossing the
lava.   Gránanes was on the other side of the Svatá,
just by a spot where the water falls ten or fifteen feet
over a hard ledge of rock extending across the river.
Beyond the river all was moraine matter, great
moraine hills, the material of which has come down
from Hoff Jökull and has been piled up for miles
along its margins.   Many very fine erratics are
dotted about on the surface near Gránanes.

   It was on the moraine side of the river that we

made our camp. Round about there was lying a
number of twigs and dried roots, the remains of
dwarf willows that had grown there when the conditions were rather more favourable. Miss Hastie
suggested that we might be energetic and collect
some of these in order to make a fire. It was a
cold night, and the idea of a camp-fire commended

A SURVEY PHOTOGRAPH (NO. 169) FROM GRÁNANES (⊙ E)
LOOKING TOWARDS LANG JÖKULL.

itself to us. We gathered together a number of the
twigs and roots, and Hill tried to ignite them. He
raised a dense smoke, but though he worked hard
and fanned industriously he was unable to induce
a satisfactory blaze. Anyhow, it was cheering to
see the smoke rising into the air, and we did not
mind being half stifled when occasionally it was
blown into our faces.

Next morning, after breakfast, I went up to a terrace of the moraine where I made my fifth station, and fixed its position on the map; I also did some plane-tabling while preparations were being made for an expedition to Kerlingarfjöll.

CHAPTER VII

THE INTERIOR—KERLINGARFJÖLL

WHEN preparations had been completed, some of us started for the mountains of Kerlingarfjöll, where high up, among the snow and ice, there are hot springs, fumaroles, and solfataras. The party was a small one. Thomas, Hill, and I started with the conductor and two guides. Unfortunately Thomas's side was giving him "fits," and he had to return after going but a very short distance.

We had a big quicksand river, the Jokulvisl, to cross—a river that is often highly dangerous, and sometimes, when the water is "up," unfordable. We were accompanied so far by the "nautical adviser" and the "handy man," who afterwards proceeded up the river to view a very fine gorge in it, which we saw from the other side. The journey was most interesting; we crossed vast moraines, where enormous erratics were dotted about on the surface, before we reached the Jokulvisl. The guides all had a great dread of this river; but we made a good crossing, for the recent cold weather had retarded the melting of the snow, and there was no flood in the river, though it was running very

swiftly. The sensation when crossing these swift-
running rivers is very uncanny—one seems to be
rushing up-stream against the current, and on looking at the ponies and their riders in front the
impression is deepened: they seem to be moving
rapidly as the water rushes by and foams round
them, but really the pace is very slow, for the ponies

A SURVEY PHOTOGRAPH (NO. 183) TAKEN FROM ⊙ F LOOKING TOWARDS
KERLINGARFJÖLL.

plod along steadily through the water. Even if
those in front could be ignored, the impression of
going rapidly up-stream could not be effaced, for the
water would rush by and swirl round one's own pony
just the same. It might be thought that a glance
at the opposite bank of the river ought to dispel
the illusion, but even that does not correct the
false impression. After crossing the Jokulvisl, we

proceeded along its banks for nearly a mile to where the river has carved its way deep down through the lava, and left sides that rise vertically for a hundred feet or more. There is a fine hard dyke in one place extending into the river, on the end of which a pinnacle rises that adds much to the grandeur of the scene. After photographing this gorge, we proceeded across more moraine matter until reach-

ASCENDING A SNOW SLOPE.

ing some of the main blocks of the Kerlingarfjöll mountains. In these moraines we had very steep slopes to ascend and descend; in one case the descent was so sharp that for safety we all dismounted and led our ponies down the side, at each step sending down a shower of stones and pebbles. At Kerlingarfjöll we suddenly came upon a series of inclined snow-fields, one of which we ascended, traversing it from end to end. It was more than a

mile long, but the zigzag course that we had to
pursue made it seem almost interminable; as it
was, we were nearly an hour making the crossing.
The photograph shows the members of the party
apparently soaring up to heaven on their ponies,
who in their wild flight seem to be emulating
Pegasus. Soon after we had started up this snow
slope, the clouds descended upon us and we were
enveloped in a thick mist; we could see nothing

KERLINGARFJÖLL—FIRE AND ICE.

but just a very limited circle of snow around us,
and thus we proceeded, zigzagging the whole way.
We crossed several other snow-fields, but they were
of less extent.

When approaching the hot springs, we became
aware of their nearness by the sulphurous smell that
came wafting towards us. Suddenly, from a ridge,
we beheld a most wonderful and awe-inspiring sight.
All around there were snow- and ice-fields, and from
their midst, but on the far side of a deep valley

that intervened, there rose a cloud of steam, the strong sulphurous smell of which suggested the nearness of the lower regions. There was a mass of yellow, brown, green, and blue clayey matter— liparite softened by steam it was—that had been cut and shaped by ice, snow, and water into a series of cones and cone-like surfaces, and from crevices in this clay the sulphurous steam escaped. Below was the deep intervening valley, the valley of the Ásquidsá, a river that flows from the upper heights of Kerlingarfjöll. To get down to this stream was a work of no slight difficulty; it required patience, much hard work, and much coaxing of ponies. We rode through the snow, and slid down steep slopes of various-coloured clay. These slopes became so precipitous at last that we all had to dismount and plod along their sides, coaxing our unwilling steeds to follow. Presently we reached what looked very much like an *impasse* at the end of a valley, the sides of which had gradually converged until the channel was then scarcely wider than the ponies were broad. The guides were not to be beaten, however, for they proceeded on foot, and literally dragged the ponies one by one down this channel, to where the snow came to an end and there was a drop of two or three feet into a small stream of water. The guides splashed into this, and by dint of much coaxing induced the ponies to follow, leading them along the stream. Right at the end there was a small waterfall, with a deep pool below. Down the fall they slid, splashing into the pool, where they stood panting beside the main stream that we had seen from above, which ran at right angles to the smaller stream. Meantime, Hill, the conductor, and I had been walking at a slightly higher level on the top of a gradually descending spur of clayey matter. Down the slope of this we scrambled on all fours, carrying with us several pounds' weight of the clay on each boot, to say nothing of what we had on clothes and hands. From the side of the steep slope we mounted our ponies, considerably heavier than when we had been on their backs a few minutes before. We crossed the stream to the hot springs. Some of the ponies objected to passing the hot, steaming holes, and absolutely refused for a long time to do so; but eventually all were coaxed or dragged by. To describe the place is impossible, and mere words are inadequate to explain the nature of the scene. Photographs that I took do not give much idea of the place, for they are all more or less failures. It differs from anything that I saw in New Zealand, because in the hot spring region in the North Island there is no ice and snow. I took a boiling-point observation for altitude, and found the elevation of the stream at the foot of the burning hill to be 3088 feet above sea-level.

I hurried over lunch, and set off with Hannes, one of the guides, to try to do some plane-tabling; but the Fates, in the shape of dense mist, were against me, and prevented me from seeing anything more distant than a few hundred feet. On the up-ward journey I had noticed a good position for a new station. On the way down to the spot chosen, which was below the long snow slope, we mistook our way in the mist, and went down the wrong slope, coming to an almost sheer descent before

finding out our mistake. We learnt this just in time,
however, to prevent a catastrophe. We retraced our
steps by the tracks in the snow, until we reached
the right slope, and there struck the zigzag track
made on the ascent. The intended new station was
reached without further incident occurring.

From the glimpses of the country that I had
obtained on the upward journey, I was convinced
that to make a map of these mountains (Kerlingarfjöll) would require a week of fine weather and
a series of camps on the spot. As nothing of much
value could be done in a few hours, I did not lose
very much by the mist having descended over the
country, except the exceedingly fine views. It was
disappointing not to be able to get to work with
camera, but under the circumstances nothing could
be done except growl at adverse luck.

After waiting an hour or so for the rest of
the party—Hill, the conductor, and Sigurthur—who
came on more at their leisure, we resumed the descent
towards the plains. Suddenly we got below the line
of drifting clouds, and there we beheld some wonderful sights—remarkable scenes due to a series of
rapid atmospheric changes. A small lake in the lava-
field suddenly came into view as we reached the
line of the reflected sunlight. The lake shone out,
gradually increasing in intensity, until it glowed
brilliantly with a marvellous light. The effect as
the scene opened out beneath the clouds was weirdly
wonderful. Some of the clouds were of a deep blue,
almost purple, tint, producing, as they overhung a
line of bright light and vivid colouring, a most impressive picture. Away in the distance, on Lake

Hvítarvatn, we could see icebergs floating in their hundreds. These bergs were great blocks of ice that had broken away from the glaciers flowing from Lang Jökull into the lake. The return journey was accomplished, without the occurrence of any untoward incident, at a rate that showed of what stuff the ponies were made, for they cantered over the roughest of moraines with scarcely a stumble, and we made excellent time to our camp at Gránanes. There we found that a real fire had been conjured up in our absence, and a successful attempt made to bake bread in a wash-hand basin—an instance of the shifts that had to be made, which were many and various.

When passing over the sloping moraine matter towards Kerlingarfjöll we crossed a number of peculiar terrace formations, and we often found similar terraces on the hillsides in other places also. These terraces have edges or banks of vegetation, which seem to grow in irregular lines and to arrest the natural descent of alluvial matter, forming a series of terraces or steps that rise, as a rule, but a few inches one above another. The vegetation also collects some of the wind-blown sand of the deserts, which thus assists in the formation of the terraces.

CHAPTER VIII

I WAS early at work next morning, and did some plane-tabling at Gránanes before breakfast. Afterwards, when I had finished what I wanted to do at that station, Thomas and I, accompanied by Thorlakur, the guide, proceeded to Efriskutur, a mountain four or five miles distant, on the highest point of which I purposed making my sixth station. We rode down the river and along the ridge of a long stretch of moraine where there were some fine "erratics"; one very large specimen being worthy of a photograph, I got Thorlakur on horseback to stand beside it while I took a record with camera. Along these moraines we went until reaching the slopes of Efriskutur, up which we rode to the summit. I set up the table on the highest point, and got to work; but the sorrows of a plane-tabler were very marked. A strong wind was blowing, and my first trouble was when, in an unguarded moment, I had my hand off the paper; the wind, a very cold and strong one, caught up the map and tore it from the pins by which it was fastened to the table; it was being whisked away, when Thomas caught it, and so pre-

80

vented it from disappearing on the wings of half a
gale into the valley several hundred feet below. I
next found that my tracing-paper had gone, and that
it was impossible to use paper of any kind to work
out the position of the new station, for the wind was
altogether too strong for it to be held down on
the map. I got out some drawing-paper, however,
in readiness for an attempt, and in a bit of a lull in

IMMENSE "ERRATICS."

the wind I managed, by cutting holes along the lines
of sight, to find the position—it had not been fixed
from other stations, for there was only one ray to it.
We were nearly frozen by the intense coldness of the
wind that was blowing straight from the ice of Lang
Jökull, but fortunately it abated slightly after a while
and enabled me to get to work. Lunch soon afterwards, and the reappearance of the sun, tended to
restore better circulation, and thenceforward all went

well, except that when I wanted to make a boiling-point observation for altitude, the water-bottle was found to be empty. I had lent it to Hill the previous day at the Kerlingarfjöll hot springs in order that he might collect algæ; he had returned it empty, and I had forgotten to refill it. As we had brought no water with us for lunch, it looked as if the observation could not be made for want of it; but I remembered in time that there was a small patch of snow on the mountain-side, not very far down. Thomas kindly went to get some of the snow, which I melted, and was thus enabled to complete the observation. Efriskutur is a tuff mountain; at first we supposed that it was composed entirely of moraine matter, for on the Kerlingarfjöll side, by which we ascended, the hill is covered with it. On examining the other side there was no trace of moraine; there was scree in places, but a great deal of the tuff was uncovered. When the atmosphere was quite clear in the afternoon, we saw standing out above the ice of Lang Jökull a prominent peak, a fine specimen of a volcanic neck.

Our work done, we made tracks for Hvitarvatn, the lake beside which we were to camp that night. To the river Svartá we traversed moraine matter; beyond the river, however, which we crossed, there was no moraine—nothing but the recent lava from Strytur, which quite covered the intervening country to the Falakvisl, a river that has carved its way along the other edge of the lava; on the far side there are great moraine hills. The Falakvisl is a deep, swift river, flowing between banks that are very high in places; it drains the valley between

the ice of Lang Jökull and the outlying range north
of the mountain Hrutafell, round which it flows,
collecting the streams that run down from it and
from the other mountains and hills south of the
divide of Kjalhraun, the lava ridge by Strytur.   This
river discharges its waters into Lake Hvitarvatn,
and we followed its course to within a mile or so of
the point of discharge.

We found the camp beside the lake, about a mile
from the water; there was no convenient camping-
ground any nearer to it, for the intervening land was
a mere swamp.   We were in the midst of wonderful
and magnificent surroundings.   The lake was covered
with innumerable icebergs—great lumps broken off
from the edges of two great glaciers that flow from
Lang Jökull to the water's edge on the far side of the
lake.   It was interesting to note the fact that the
farther away the icebergs were from the glaciers the
smaller they were, until on the margin of the lake
where the water was not so cold they disappeared
altogether.   Facing us was a great basaltic mountain,
Skrutharfell, set in between the two fine glaciers
mentioned.   To the left was the great solid mass of
Bláfell (pronounced Blou-fettle, the á like ou in
blouse), a mountain that had much snow covering
its sides; to the right, Hrutafell reared its icy head
high into the air; behind, there was the mountain
range of Kerlingarfjöll.   All this was affected by
the gorgeousness of the sunset effects; the sun was
descending behind the ice-flow, and lighting up ice
and snow with the most wonderful colouring; it was
a thing to be seen and remembered—to describe it in
adequate terms is impossible.

The lake was the resort of many swans, which disturbed the slumbers of at least one member of the party, for they called and squawked in the most persistent manner through the small hours—I will not say of the night, for we were having twenty-four hours of daylight just then.

I was moving early next morning, for I intended to get to work at the plane-table, but the Fates were against me once more, this time in the shape of clouds which overhung the tops of Kerlingarfjöll and Hrutafell, completely hiding two of the points of those mountains that I required to sight in order to fix my position. I set up the plane-table, however, in the hope that the clouds would clear later on, and then took a boiling-point observation. After breakfast I waited in vain for an hour or two for the clouds to rise and the peaks to clear, for otherwise it was impossible to fix the position. The peaks *were* gradually clearing, but time was passing; we had a long day's journey before us, and a deep and dangerous river to ford on the way, so a guide could not well be spared to wait an hour or two until proper observations were possible. I had to make the best of it, so took sights on a separate sheet of paper to a number of points, hoping that eventually I should be able to complete. The peaks *did* clear at the last moment, and I took sights to them; but as there was not time to fix the position on the map itself and to take the other sights again, I did all that was possible under the circumstances, hoping that what had been done would fit in properly. On returning to England, I found the observations agreed very well with my previous work.

My work, so far as the map was concerned, was at an end. I cannot say that it was completed, for the time spent there was too short to permit of the whole of the country lying between Lang Jökull and Hoff Jökull being mapped. I had hoped to complete a map extending from Dufufell and Hveravellir in the north to the mountains of Kerlingarfjöll and the lake of Hvitarvatn to the south; but several things conspired to prevent my doing it full justice, the chief of which were that we were two days late in arriving at Hveravellir, and that the weather was not quite so good as it might have been.

It was about mid-day, if I remember rightly, when we got under way and proceeded along near the shore of the lake; we crossed the Svartá close by where it enters the lake, and at a point just below where the river falls over a ledge of hard rock ten to twelve feet high. We passed over great accumulations of moraine matter towards Blâfell, gradually rising until an excellent view of Hvitarvatn and the myriads of icebergs floating on its surface was obtained. So we proceeded until we came to the river Hvitá. This was one of our big rivers, and its crossing was a dangerous undertaking. The pack, as usual, showed the way and made a successful crossing. We stayed behind, for the purpose of photographing the pack when in mid-stream. The photograph that I took shows the pack-train right in the middle of the river. We followed, and crossed without any untoward incident occurring; the water was rather deep, and when in mid-stream it came up to our knees. At this river we saw a number of sheep swimming across, which is quite a common thing for them to do.

I afforded some entertainment to my companions in the course of the day. The pony I was then riding was a confirmed stumbler, and he blundered along during the whole day, sometimes on four legs, but more often on three; occasionally he shortened his two front legs and tried to make good time on his knees. It was not altogether pleasant riding, for

THE PACK-TRAIN CROSSING THE HVITÁ.

there was great uncertainty as to which mode of progression he would next adopt. After several bad stumbles he came to grief. He stumbled, recovered, went on two paces, and then came right down. He caught me off guard when having a loose seat immediately after his recovery, with the result that I was deposited, very nicely and quietly, however, in a soft sand-patch that was handy. I was much disgusted, for I happened to be just in front of the other members of the party. But this was nothing compared with the next entertainment that I gave soon afterwards. We had not proceeded much farther before some of the rotten saddlery gave way: my crupper broke and a ring at the back of the saddle was dragged out—my oilskins, etc., came adrift and fell; but one of the packages did not get free, it hung by a strong cord at the pony's heels, where it dangled, knocking against them. My pony did what any self-respecting pony would have done in similar circumstances — he promptly bolted! Now the ground thereabouts was not remarkable for its evenness; indeed, it was one of the roughest pieces of ground that we passed over in the course of the day. He made excellent time, and the harder he went, the more the package hit against his heels, until he became quite frantic with fright and ran amuck. I was at the rear of the party some distance behind when he started off, but we soon caught up the others, bumping into one, cannoning off a second to a third, and nearly unseating Miss Hastie, who was not prepared for the charge. My only fear, as he was such a bad stumbler and had already been down, was that he would come a cropper in the course of his wild career and throw me upon a lump of lava; but as he kept his feet, I stuck to him and at last managed to get him under control and pull him up. He stood trembling in affright, for the objectionable package was still at his heels. I dismounted and removed the disturbing cause, afterwards returning in company with the "handy man" to collect the goods and chattels that were lying distributed over the country that had just

been crossed in something like record time.   In spite
of the bumps and knocks that they received, my
companions enjoyed the spectacle, and it afforded
them an opportunity for some good-natured chaff.

During the latter part of the day's journey, which
was along the high banks of the river Hvitá, we saw
some fair specimens of columnar basalt.   There were

A FINE GORGE IN THE SIDE OF BLÁFELL.

times, when we were travelling along on the edge of
these high banks within a few inches of the edge of
a drop of two or three hundred feet, that I did not
feel quite comfortable, for my pony continued to
stumble along to the end of the journey ; but he did
not come right down again, though several times he
had to be pulled up from his knees.

We came round Bláfell in the course of the day,
and there saw a number of very fine gorges in the

GULLFOSS—FRONT VIEW WITH "RAINBOW" EFFECT.

GULLFOSS—SIDE VIEW.

GULLFOSS—THE UPPER FALL.

GULLFOSS—THE UPPER FALL.

upon the very striking mountains that fringe its
edge, the Jarlhettur (the Earl's Hats) as they are
called, because of the shapes of their upper portions;
several of these peaks are interesting inasmuch as
they are, without doubt, the hard cores of ancient
volcanoes—volcanic plugs or necks.

At Sandá we remained over Sunday, but as it

GULLFOSS—THE FALL INTO THE RAVINE.

rained hard we were confined to our tents nearly the
whole day—our Sundays were, as a rule, very wet,
and of six or seven that we had in or about Iceland
only two were fine; it did not matter much, for
Sunday with us was always a day of rest, and the
rain only kept us to our tents.   On these occasions
much tobacco was consumed and as many matches
were used as economy allowed.

On leaving Sandá our way lay for several miles over

a desolate sandy and stony desert. Farther on there were many evidences of ice-action : the rounded forms of boulders attracted our attention, as did numerous ice-scratchings on them ; some of the outcropping lumps were beautifully rounded, and in one place (in

GULLFOSS—THE RAVINE BELOW THE FALLS.

the same valley as Gullfoss) after passing the falls, but just before reaching Bratholt, there was undoubted evidence that the ice had swept up a slight rise in the valley before descending the steep slope towards the Bratholt farm.

Gullfoss is one of the sights of Iceland. It is a magnificent waterfall on the Hvitá, where the white

water of the river cascades over a series of step-like
barriers stretching from side to side, and then plunges
finally over a ledge of very hard rock into a yawning
abyss more than a hundred feet deep, whence it throws
up clouds of spray that are carried hither and thither
as the wind sweeps first this way and then that; so
thick is the spray, that one's clothing soon becomes

BELOW GULLFOSS—CASTELLATED DYKES.

saturated on incautiously getting into it. Gullfoss is
one of the finest waterfalls in Europe, and it is only
surpassed in grandeur, if at all, by one or two others
in Iceland. We saw the falls at their best, for when
we arrived the sun was shining brightly and a rainbow playing over the spray as it rose from the gorge.
It is true that the sky clouded over afterwards, and
that rain began to fall before we left Gullfoss, but
we carried away the impression of the broken waters

of the cascade sparkling in the sun, and of the colours of the rainbow playing on the spray over the ravine. The water has carved out a deep gorge in the basalt, and below the falls there are many good specimens of basaltic columns. In the lower part of the gorge there are the picturesque remains of a very fine hard dyke that has a much softer one beside it. These remains are to be seen on both sides of the river, and they have assumed the outline and form of a number of castellated buildings perched high upon prominent peaks.

CHAPTER IX

WE were very near the margin of the desert interior, for within two or three miles we arrived at the farm-house of Bratholt, the first human habitation that we had seen for ten or twelve days. We had traversed the uninhabited country and were then entering upon the final stage of the journey across the island, where we expected to see some of the better class of farms and farmers. Bratholt farm-house seemed to be one of the superior kind—it was certainly the best that we had seen so far. We lunched there, and while the meal was being prepared were shown over the premises by the farmer's wife and daughters. A fine specimen of an old kitchen attracted my attention, and I determined to try to photograph it. The housewife was most anxious to help with the camera. I had a difficulty in setting it up in a suitable position, so she volunteered to hold it wherever I wanted it to stand. I tried to explain that she could not hold it still enough, and that it would have to be kept in one position for nearly ten minutes; she stood in the way looking on till I fetched a guide to explain matters, when she left me to my own devices. It was quite a picture, this kitchen; one of the curiosities it contained was an old quern with a bone (human?) for a handle. The room was as smoky as most of the Icelandic kitchens usually are; in the roof there was a number of skins that had been hung up to dry or placed there for preservation. Some three-legged pots stood in a corner on the floor; a fire was burning in a fireplace built of lumps of basalt, and the smoke that arose from the smouldering peat bricks hung in the air till it gradually escaped through a hole in the roof.

We invaded the work-room and bed-chamber, which is usually called the *bathstofa*. As its name implies, this chamber was once the bath-room of the house; but bathing has gone much out of fashion with the Icelander, and he no longer considers a tub at short intervals to be desirable. The *bathstofa* is now used as a living-room; it is fitted up with a series of open bunks ranged along the sides, in which the various members of the family repose at night; but the bunks serve not only for sleeping purposes— they are often the receptacle for all sorts of things, and we could hardly help noticing in one a miscellaneous collection consisting of sugar, stockings, skin shoes, tea, etc. There were several spinning-wheels in the room, and at our request the lady of the house set to work at one of them. The family made cloth, various articles of clothing from it, sheep-skin shoes, and bone spoons with "Gullfoss" carved on them, for the "trippers" who call when on the way to Gullfoss. One of the daughters was an expert in the use of vegetable dyes; she was not at home, but we saw some of her work. We bought a few things: shoes, stockings, gloves, rugs, etc., and the "handy

man" cleared out the stock of cloth and called for
more, but more was not to be had there. Later in
the day, however, we passed another farm where
cloth could sometimes be bought; the "handy man"
heard of this, and we lost sight of him for more than
an hour while he was, ostensibly, making further
purchases, though he did not seem to be over-
burdened with their weight when at last he turned
up. In the evening he remarked on the beauty of
a girl that he had seen at the farm, which raised
grave doubts as to whether the charms of this beauty
had not been the *real* cause of his long stay there.
We thought it mean of him not to have informed
us when in the neighbourhood, and told him so; he
smiled serenely, for we were then a safe distance
away—half a day's journey. We expected to camp
that night at Geysir; so when the "handy man"
appeared with his bundle of cloth, we pushed on for
that interesting spot. We had to cross the river
Tungufljot on the way; it is a rather deep and swift-
flowing river, but we made an excellent crossing at
a recently discovered ford where the water did not
reach much above the level of our stirrups.

At Geysir there is a region of hot springs, geysers,
and blue, boiling cauldrons, where one can stand on
the sinter margins, look deep down into the blue
waters, and imagine whence they come. There is
also a number of holes where liquid mud bubbles and
splutters. There are geysers active, and others quiescent and extinct. Among the latter is the celebrated
Strokur—a few years ago it was very active, but now
it is quite dead; it died during an earthquake that
occurred in 1896. Although the earthquake stopped

Strokur, it seems to have caused Great Geysir itself to play with increased energy. Strokur had to be coaxed into activity, but it was easily done by feeding it with lumps of turf, which were thrown into its yawning mouth, wide open always and ready for a meal. It never failed to give a display when properly fed. It was when it had had a surfeit, and was likely to be choked with the turf, that it erupted, ejecting the turf violently, and at the same time shooting upward a column of boiling water and steam. But all this is of the past—no quantity of turf will provoke it into activity now; it is dead, and there is no indication that it was once the scene of violent disturbance; nothing remains as a record of former glories but a hole in the ground a few feet in diameter.

It was late in the evening when we arrived. The weather was not what we should have liked, for it was dull and rainy; there had been much rain at Geysir during the previous few days, and we were informed of the fact by a farmer living in the neighbourhood. It is said that Geysir erupts more frequently during and after a period of much rain, and also when the wind blows from a certain quarter —I forget which quarter, but that is immaterial now, for the all-important thing is that it was then blowing in the favourable direction. Whether there is any real ground for the reports I do not know, but I record the fact that during a stay of about fourteen hours Geysir erupted six times, and that the average is said to be one in twenty-four hours. The first eruption occurred while we were at supper at about 10.15 P.M. There was a dull, deep-seated thud somewhere below, a sort of subterranean rumbling that

caused us to inquire of our conductor, who was rather
deaf, what it was. We had previously been informed
that certain premonitory rumblings always preceded
an eruption ; but we were doubtful whether what we
then heard was the warning. The conductor had not
heard it, and he was endeavouring to explain to us
the nature of the sound when a guide rushed to the
door of the tent to inform us that Geysir was about
to play. We hastily left our meal, made an abrupt
exit from the tent, and rushed to the spot. Surely
enough it was in eruption, for great clouds of steam
were rising from the crater and rolling towards us.
We got to windward of the steam, and looked
towards the crater, and what a sight it was ! High
into the air, sixty, seventy, eighty feet up, there was
shooting stream after stream of boiling water, which
fell in showers of spray all around, some descending
towards the crater and meeting on its way the out-
going streams. A ring of sinter surrounds the crater ;
it is raised ten to fifteen feet above the general level
of the ground, so the hot water that fell upon it ran
off in a ring of little cascades. It was a wonderful
sight, this enormous natural fountain ; it continued
to play for two or three minutes before it gradually
subsided and stopped—all was then still, save that
the last of the water was streaming over the edges of
the sinter ring, whence a little steam was rising. As
soon as the eruption came to an end, we climbed upon
the ring, which has a diameter of something like a
hundred feet ; there is a large depression or basin in
it that is filled with water before eruption, but it was
then empty. In the middle of the basin there is a
funnel, said to be about sixty feet deep ; at the

surface it is about sixteen feet in diameter. We stood on the edge of this funnel or crater, looking down into its depths, the water then standing at a level of something like fifteen feet below that at which we had previously seen it.

We returned to our interrupted meal, congratulating ourselves that we had arrived just in time to

THE SINTER RING OF GEYSIR.

witness the fine display, without at all expecting that we should have another opportunity of seeing such a spectacle. But, as I have stated, we were lucky enough to see in all six eruptions, three of which occurred at short intervals during the night. The first occurred at 10.15 P.M.; the others at 1.30, 3.30, 6.30, 8.30, and the last of the series at 10.45 A.M. The finest displays were the first, second, and last. The second, that at 1.30 A.M., occurred just after we had turned in, but the warning rumblings sounded before we had gone to sleep. Each made a dash at some articles of clothing, and hastening into them, made a blind rush through the rain to the side of Geysir, where we presented a curious spectacle : we were a very motley assemblage indeed, and the various costumes it would perhaps · be better not to

THE FUNNEL OR CRATER OF GEYSIR.

describe accurately. I have not a photographic record of the scene—there had been no time to get out cameras, and the light was very bad.

There is a smaller geyser, known as Little Geysir, distant about a quarter of a mile from its more important neighbour. Now, this happened to be in good working order, for it erupted while we were finishing our evening meal, sending up spray to a height of from ten to twenty feet, and

continued more or less active during the rest of the
night.

Many were the boiling and bubbling springs that
we saw along a line of fissure nearly half a mile in
extent. The basins of some of them were very
beautiful, one especially, where the water was of a
bright blue colour and the edges of the sinter basin
quite white. The basins and terraces are composed
of the silica that was at one time held in solution in
the water that flowed over them; it was gradually
deposited layer upon layer, slowly lining the vent
through which the water was ejected, and building
up the terraces and basins.

We were loth to leave the neighbourhood of Geysir
and continue on our way; but we could not linger,
because time was of importance to some of the
members of the party, who had to reach Reykjavik,
the capital of the country, in time to catch a certain
steamer. Another day could not be spared, so on we
had to go. We proceeded at first over a quantity of
sinter debris, and then through some hummocky land.
After a while we came to a wood—an Icelandic forest,
or one of the nearest approaches to a forest that Iceland can boast. It consisted of a quantity of scrubby
birch and willow "trees," mere bushes, averaging
three to five feet in height, though some, it is true,
attained the height of six or even seven feet;
interspersed amongst them were some geraniums
(*G. silvaticum*). The river Bruará flows through the
middle of the wood, and we had to cross it on our
way. The crossing was a peculiar one. At the spot
there is a rapid in the river, with a waterfall just
below. Hard rock stretches from side to side, forming

a barrier that is cleft in the middle of the river; the water flows with very picturesque effect over the ledge and into the cleft, which is bridged by a wooden platform; the crossing is effected by the bridge, and by fording the river on each side of it. While I was photographing the spot with some members of the party on the bridge, my pony ran away, and crossed the river, leaving me on the wrong side of it.   However, the runaway did not get very far before its career was checked; it was then brought back, and I followed in the track of the others.

Farther on in the wood we halted at a wayside farm-house for lunch, and to rest for a while before continuing on what was likely to be a long journey. Away we went again, though, through the wood, until we overlooked the Bruará at a spot where it had worn down the valley to the level of a plain of denudation, of which it is a fine specimen.   There, below, was the river meandering in a winding course over the plain; there also were two small lakes, one of which, Laugarvatn, is of historical interest, for it was there that the Icelanders on being converted to Christianity were baptized; they objected to cold water, but a hot spring in this lake causes the water to be warm, so the objection was overcome, and they were baptized in the warm waters of Laugarvatn. We gradually descended to the vicinity of Laugarvatn-shellirar, a peculiar volcanic district, where a number of castellated-looking rocks on the hillsides are very suggestive of ancient ruins.   To the left of them rises the Kalfstindar range, the peaks of which are the hard plugs of ancient volcanoes that have become exposed by the erosion of the softer material of the

original cones. Here we came upon recent lava
again, and during the rest of the day's journey we
were obliged to travel very slowly, for we had to
pick our way over very rough ground.

The ponies stumbled along hour after hour, much
to the discomfiture of the "nautical adviser," who
was in a helpless state, suffering great pain. Earlier
in the day he had been stung on the eye by an insect.
At first he did not feel much inconvenience, but as
time passed, his eye became inflamed and very
troublesome; so intense was the pain at last, that
his eyes had to be bandaged. Thus blindfolded he
had to ride on, just balancing himself, and allowing
his pony to pick its own way through the lava as it
followed one or another of us. It was a very dangerous proceeding, because the lava over which he had
to pass was of the roughest possible kind; the ponies
had to perform all sorts of peculiar antics while dodging
from side to side, or in climbing over boulders or out-
cropping rocks, now going up a steep slope, then
descending one at a dangerous-looking angle. When
three or four miles from Thingvellir, our destination
that night, we came to a great rift in the earth
known as Hrafna-gjá (Raven's Rift), a crack going
deep down into the earth, and extending three or
four miles in a line parallel to another even greater
rift that will be again referred to. On reaching
Hrafna-gjá, we had to climb down its steep side,
there being a drop of something like a hundred feet
to the lava at its foot. The steepness and uneven-
ness of the descent rendered it necessary for us all to
dismount and lead our ponies down. The day was
dull and the light then becoming bad; but we had

to plod on. We were not many miles from our destination, Thingvellir. We presently saw right ahead what looked like a line of high precipitous cliffs with a white patch in it. At first we were very doubtful what the patch could be; but on drawing nearer we heard the splash of falling water, and from the sound, judged that the volume was pretty large. We could see nothing distinctly, though, for it was approaching midnight and the light was failing fast, so we pushed on along a line parallel to the cliff, unable to distinguish anything clearly.

It was at Vallholt, close to the margin of Lake Thingvallavatn, that we halted. There we reached modern civilisation suddenly, for we came to a large galvanised iron structure which we found to be a hotel, so we pulled up and dismounted. On inquiring for our tents, we were informed that they had not been erected, and that we were to take up our quarters at the hotel. We had not expected this, and as we had all become somewhat attached to our canvas quarters, we grumblingly entered the hotel and went in search of our boxes. The arrangement of the interior was peculiar: a large hall occupied the middle of the building, extending the full width, and reaching from floor to roof; at each end of the hall, a passage led through to the end of the building. On each side of one of these passages there was ranged a number of cabin-like rooms, each of which contained two bunks, one above the other, and in a corner there was a wash-hand basin, the whole being fitted up like the interior of a cabin on board ship—this was accounted for by the fact that the arrangement had been designed by a sailor.

Thomas and I had piloted the "nautical adviser" and given his pony a lead during the last part of the journey, so we three were rather late in our arrival; but we were met with the cheering intelligence that supper (it was 11.30 P.M.) would be ready in a few minutes, and that we were to "hurry up" and make whatever change of costume we deemed necessary to celebrate the return to some of the conventionalities of modern civilisation. We were hungry, very hungry, and did not waste time over an elaborate toilet, but soon put in an appearance in the large central hall. Here we were regaled with a most sumptuous and excellent banquet. The soup was all that could be desired, and it was hot—a very comforting thing when one is half frozen. This whetted our appetite for the other good things that were to follow: salmon that was cooked to perfection; then came another excellent dish, and last of all delicious pastry and cream —the Icelanders, as I have already stated, are noted for the quality of their pastry. We had growled on finding that we were to take up quarters in a tourists' hotel, but the quality of the dinner quite reconciled us to the return to civilisation. We had been living for more than a fortnight on tinned foods, so we fully appreciated the good things that "mine host" had provided for us. We were disappointed in one way; but when a hungry man has fed well he is not disposed to quarrel with things in general—especially when they take the form of a fairly comfortable bunk and more room in his cabin than he would have had in his tent.

Thingvellir and the neighbourhood is a most

interesting and historic place, for it was there, in the tenth century, that the Althing, or Parliament, used to assemble. The spot whereon it once met, known as the Logberg (Law Rock), is now a verdure-covered hill, lying between two remarkable rifts in the lava. Thingvallavatn is the name of the largest and most picturesque lake in Iceland; the view of it which we had obtained the day before from above Hrafna-gjá was very fine, but the atmosphere had not been quite clear; we had seen enough, however, in spite of rain and haze, to enable us to form an idea of the beauty of the scene. We were favoured on this occasion, for the air was clearer and the light brighter, so we were better able, from the elevated site of the Logberg, to enjoy the fine view. The meeting-place of the Althing was removed from the Logberg to one of two islands lying in the lake, but to which of them is questionable, though it is supposed that it used to meet on the long flat island near Thingvellir, close to the shore of the lake.

Not only is this neighbourhood interesting historic-ally, but geologically it claims attention. I have already mentioned the remarkable rift, Hrafna-gjá; there is another at Thingvellir—I am not referring to the two rifts at the Logberg, for though notice-able in themselves, they are but minor rifts when compared with that of Hrafna-gjá, and still more so when comparison is made with Almanna-gjá (All-men's Rift) at Thingvellir. It is a most extraordinary break in the earth, extending for three or four miles across the country in a line parallel to Hrafna-gjá, showing a face of lava with a drop of something like a hundred feet. Now what has happened to cause

these extraordinary rifts? The whole of the land
between Hrafna-gjá and Almanna-gjá has fallen in,
dropped through about a hundred feet, and forms a
" rift valley." The lake derives its water chiefly by
underground rivers from the ice-field of Lang Jökull,
though one small stream, the Oxará, runs into it.
This river tumbles over the edge of the cliffs by a

ALMANNA-GJÁ—IN THE RIFT NEAR THE WATERFALL.

fine cascade into the rift of Almanna-gjá; but it
does not flow very far (less than a mile) before it
escapes through a gap in the outer wall of the rift
by a second and smaller fall. Above the smaller
fall there is a pool known as the Murderesses' Pool,
in which it was once the custom to drown women
found guilty of infanticide or adultery.

There are several legends connected with Thingvellir. One of them refers to a remarkable jump

supposed to have been performed by one Flossi, an
outlaw, who, on being closely pursued, escaped by
jumping across one of the lava rifts of the Logberg
hill—an impossible feat with the rift at its present
width, but it is supposed to have widened considerably.   In these rifts of the Logberg there is, deep
down, some beautifully clear water standing at about
the same level as the lake.   Over one of the rifts
there is a small wooden bridge with a hole in the
middle of it; beside the hole we saw a bucket with
a long rope attached.   As the clear water of one
of the pools was immediately below, it was not difficult to infer that this was the source of the water-
supply of the hotel which was in the immediate
neighbourhood.

After we had seen all that was of special interest
at Thingvellir, we started on the last stage of our
journey across the island; but before doing so we
took leave of two of the guides, Josef and Sigurthur,
who were returning to our starting-point, Akureyri,
with about a dozen of the ponies; for we had no
further use for the full pack, seeing that we expected
to reach Reykjavik, the capital, in the course of a
few hours.   From this place to Reykjavik a road has
been constructed—a rough one at best, but still a
road; the only one of any length in all Iceland,
for it is thirty-six miles long.   It commences just
below the lower fall of the Oxará; after a short
ascent, a bridge crosses the river between the waterfall and the Murderesses' Pool, whence it rises by a
steep ascent to the level of the country above the
rift.   This part of the road has been cut in the
side of the fissure of Almanna-gjá.   From above we

obtained a fine view overlooking Lake Thingvallavatn, but after losing sight of the lake we saw no more of the picturesque until nearing Reykjavik. An exceedingly fine specimen of a glaciated lava surface attracted Thomas and myself. My photograph shows it excellently : in it there can be seen the undulating surfaces of lava, the *roches moutonnées*, just as they

GLACIATED LAVA SURFACE NEAR THINGVELLIR.

were smoothed by the passing ice, and there on the surfaces are several " perched blocks " which helped in the smoothing and scratching process. There was evidence all along the road not only of the work of frost and ice, but also of that of fire and heat, for we saw in all directions tuff and lava cones and volcanic necks.

On nearing Reykjavik we met a number of pack-trains conveying goods of all descriptions to the farms. It was just the end of the season when the farmers make their annual journey to the capital. They take in their wool, dispose of it, and then return with whatever goods they have purchased. Some of the farmer's women-folk accompany him as a rule. The women ride their ponies on a saddle peculiar to Iceland. They balance themselves on their ponies seated sideways, with feet resting on a little platform that hangs suspended from the saddle by two straps; they ride by balance alone, for there is no horn by which they can grip the saddle. All goods have to be transported on the backs of ponies, for as there are no roads (with the exception of that from Reykjavik to Thingvellir) so there are no carts or waggons in general use—I did see *three* carts in Iceland, one of them in Reykjavik, but they were used only for hauling goods from the wharves into the towns. Timber and galvanised iron are carried balanced on the backs of ponies, the galvanised iron having to be doubled up. A pony sometimes looks very peculiar as he plods along with an unwieldy load swinging from side to side. He has an awkward time of it whenever there is a heavy or gusty wind blowing, and that in Iceland is very frequently. Heavy goods that cannot possibly be carried on the backs of ponies are transported when the winter snows cover the ground; rough sleighs are then used for the purpose.

CHAPTER X

THE CAPITAL—REYKJAVIK

Much to our surprise, when about two miles outside Reykjavik, we met our fellow-passenger by the *Ceres*, him with whom we had lunched at Thorshavn on the outward journey. We had left him behind at that port, and he had intended to stay for several weeks at the Faroes and to return thence to England; but having found things rather slow there, he had followed us to Iceland by the next steamer; hence the meeting on the road.

We created some sort of sensation as we entered the capital of Iceland. The clocks were striking ten as we clattered down the long main street; it was a time when the populace were at leisure and on the street, and they evinced no little curiosity as we rode by them. They were congregated in small groups, and it was evident to us that we were being discussed—and no wonder, for we were a motley-looking cavalcade! We must have presented a very grotesque appearance, clad as we were in oil-skins, and covered with mud from head to foot: it had been raining at intervals on the way, and we had had a rather disagreeable journey. We caught glimpses of faces at most of the windows peering curiously at us and watching our progress through the town. Many of the members of the groups by the wayside saluted as we passed by—the Icelanders are a polite people, as a rule, and they doff their head-gear in salutation to strangers. So we· progressed, being saluted, and acknowledging the salutes. It was a sort of triumphal entry, for the news had been carried forward by one of the guides, who was some little distance ahead with some of the pack-ponies, that we had just crossed the country by way of the uninhabited interior. All things come to an end, and so did our journey when we reached the end of the main street in Reykjavik, for there, at a great wooden building four stories high, we took up our quarters, and the crossing of Iceland was an accomplished fact.

If Reykjavik is not a town to be admired, it must be said that the surrounding scenery is most beautiful; and one of the finest sights I saw in Iceland was one evening when sunset effects were on hill and dale and over the sea.

Glasgow House—why so named we were unable to discover—was where we were quartered. The accommodation was fairly good, though there was a lack of furniture in some of the rooms. We learned that the proprietor had but lately entered into possession, and that the furniture had come from a much smaller house; it certainly required some additions to make the general accommodation equal to the table kept there. We came in hungry after our thirty-six miles' ride, so we fully appreciated the good things set before us by our hostess, a Danish. woman, who was a capable head of the kitchen. The dining-room was on the ground floor, but a steep staircase led to a large hall-like room above, from which a number of doors opened into bedrooms.

After we had eaten a most excellent meal—dinner or supper—we went for a midnight prowl round the town. Our fellow-passenger by the *Ceres*, an Oxford man, whom Thomas and I had known there, was staying at Glasgow House, so he accompanied us, and we strolled about the more retired parts away from the main street, discussing the incidents of our travels in the interior.

Reykjavik is not a very large town, as its population of about four thousand indicates. It is built on the coast and is a long, straggling place ; and although just in the business quarter there are several streets running parallel or at right angles to one another, yet, with this exception, the houses are built along the main thoroughfare. The buildings for the most part are of wooden construction, with galvanised iron roofs, though here and there a turf-roofed shanty stands as a reminder that the habitation of the average Icelander has no galvanised iron about it. Some of the principal business people are Danes, and many of the houses have been built more in conformity with Danish ideas than with those of the Icelander. The natives are fishermen and farmers, and have no very strong predilections for general business—they are inclined to leave that sort of thing to the Danes, who are more adapted to it. The clergymen and doctors are, as a rule, the sons of farmers who exhibit signs of greater brightness than the average. They first go through a course at

the Latin School, and then proceed to the Theological
College or the Medical School; some afterwards go
to Copenhagen to the University there. Both clergy
and medical men are paid by the State, though the
latter receive a nominal fee from their patients.
The finest building in Iceland is said to be the Bank
in the main street of Reykjavik. It is a strongly
built, solid-looking square structure. The ground

THE BUSINESS END OF REYKJAVIK BY THE GOVERNOR'S HOUSE.

floor is used for banking business, but the upper floor
contains a good collection of Icelandic curiosities and
antiquities—it is known as the Antiquarian Museum,
I think. Old weapons, ladies' saddles, women's
national dress, snuff and various other kinds of carved
boxes, gold and silver ornaments, altar-cloths, altar-
pieces, and other church furniture, etc., are among the
exhibits. This collection is never open to the public
in the way that similar collections are open in other

parts of the world. A visitor cannot walk in at any stated definite hour—the doors are always locked against admission unless an appointment is made with the caretaker of the collection to open them, and if, as in our case, one happens to be a little after the appointed time, a wait of half an hour while the attendant guide goes in search of the caretaker may be necessary. In the Ornithological Museum— a large room attached to a small house just away from the business part of the town—there is a fine collection of the birds of Iceland. We tried to gain admission here without having made an appointment with the caretaker, but quite failed : the door was locked, and we were unable to make known what we wanted. The only person on the premises, a middle-aged Icelandic woman, laughed and giggled and talked, and evinced no little curiosity regarding certain articles of our clothing. We thought, in our ignorance of her tongue, that she was making fun of us and of our dress. When we went away from the Museum, this woman followed us down town, and on meeting our guide we learnt that our curious friend was not quite in her right mind—a fact that accounted for her peculiar actions and manner. We saw the collection of birds on another occasion by appointment.

Facing a grassy square there are two buildings of importance—one of these, a wooden structure, is the Cathedral; the other, a massive stone building, is the Senate House, where the members of the Althing, or Parliament, meet.

Iceland has recently been granted Home Rule, but at the time of our visit the Althing consisted

of two Houses—the Upper and the Lower. The
Upper House was composed of twelve members, all
of whom were Icelanders—six of these were appointed
by the King of Denmark, the other six being elected
by the people. The Lower House consisted of
twenty-four members, all Icelanders, and all elected
by the people. Each House had a President, who

REYKJAVIK—INTERIOR OF THE CATHEDRAL.

was elected by the members. The President had no
vote, so in the Upper House the Icelanders always
tried to elect a President from the members appointed
by the King of Denmark in order to give the people's
representatives a majority of six votes to five. The
Governor, an Icelander appointed by the King, to
whom he was answerable, had the right to sit in each
House; he occupied a seat beside the presidential
chair. The members of each House were elected for

three sessions; but as the Houses met in every alternate
year only, there was an election but once in six years.
A Prime Minister was appointed by the King of
Denmark, but he did not sit in either House; in
fact, the Minister of two years ago had never been
in Iceland.   He was a Dane, residing in Copenhagen
and knowing nothing of Iceland or its requirements
except from report.   The Prime Minister resembled
our Colonial Secretary in his relations with our
Colonies, though there was a difference in that he
was *nominally* answerable to the Icelandic Althing
as well as to the King of Denmark.   Bills were
presented in either House by the whole House, by
a section of the House, or by an individual member.
The Bills were read three times, and the House might
go into Committee on a Bill at any time.   The Committee might consist of three, five, or seven members
in the Upper House—it was more often three and
five—and of three, five, seven, or nine in the Lower
House.   Either House might reject a Bill passed by
the other House.   The King of Denmark, acting on
the advice of the Icelandic Prime Minister, used to
approve a Bill passed by both Houses, when it became
law.

In the Althing there are no parties as we know
them, for all the members are united on high politics,
are republican in their feeling, and most anxious to
retain their independence of action.   The members
often have differences of opinion about a particular
Bill, of course.   The session used to last for eight
weeks only, and during that period the Houses sat
daily (Sunday excepted), often having two sittings a
day.   The members assembled at mid-day, and if the

business was not got through by four, they adjourned and met again at five. As the Althing met but once in two years, and the session was so short, there was a gap of a year and ten months when legislation was at a standstill. During that period, however, the members were often in communication one with another, and any Bills that it was desirable should be presented to the Althing at the next session were discussed in that way. The press was also the medium for the discussion of desirable legislation. As some of the members contributed to and wrote for the newspapers, the pros and cons of a particular Bill were often pretty well thrashed out before being presented to the Althing. Local affairs were managed by Sysselmen, or sheriffs, who had great powers vested in them.

When our party broke up, as it did the next day, I went on board the *Bothnia* to see off those who were leaving Iceland. The whole party had pulled so well together, and had been so successful, that we separated with feelings of regret that all could not proceed on further travels in the west of the island.

The day after the departure of those leaving Iceland, Miss Hastie and I visited Engey Island, one of the homes of the eider duck. On landing from a rowing-boat that had been hired to convey us from Reykjavik, a distance of two to three miles, we were delayed for a while by a heavy shower of rain. When it had abated we could find no one at the wharf able to speak English, so we made our way to the house of the owner of the island, for we had been informed at Reykjavik that we should find some one at Engey to point out the resorts of the ducks. We found there a young girl who could speak English very well. On learning our desires she at once offered to conduct us to the ducks, and led the way, accompanied by a sister, over a series of slippery stones and rough hummocks, to the ducks' nesting-ground. The season was almost over, so we did not see many birds in the nests. Most of the eggs had been hatched, and the parents had departed with their young, or else were swimming about in the waters around the island. Nevertheless a few birds still remained in their nests, and we found them comparatively tame; they were not quite undisturbed by our presence, though, for they moved away a few yards in an agitated state, leaving their young to blunder and stumble about all around. In vain we tried to keep the ducklings from wandering, but they would struggle out of the nest time after time, the mother walking round us the while with a watchful eye upon her brood. It is said that the down which the old birds pluck from their breasts to line the nests may be removed two or three times before they abandon them. Some of the nests, which were in the hollows between the hummocks, had bad eggs in them; so that, unless care was taken in moving from one hummock to another, a bad odour might make us aware that we had taken a false step. On returning to the house, the girls who had accompanied us showed the process of cleaning the eider-down. It is taken in handfuls and rubbed over a wire grating: the down clings to the wires, while the dirt falls through; the grating is reversed from time to time, and the down removed from the wires and rubbed repeatedly until properly cleaned and freed from dirt and foreign substances.

CHAPTER XI

WE spent two days at Reykjavik before renewing our journeyings. We were a much reduced party, for instead of eleven persons in all, we only mustered five when, on the third day from our arrival at the capital, we set out once more. Miss Hastie and myself were all that remained of the old party, but we were joined by a young Icelandic medical student, Jón Rosenkranz, while we were accompanied by our old conductor as " guide, philosopher, and friend," and Hannes as guide. Jón we soon found to be of a sportive nature, and he never seemed happier than when something was not going right. When any of the pack strayed, he seemed to be quite in his element, for he would settle into his saddle with a bump and go helter-skelter over the country after the straying ones. Hannes was his especial butt, and though Hannes himself was a mine of dry humour, yet he at times took things very seriously, and it was then that Jón was in good form; his eyes would sparkle, and he would slyly endeavour to "take a rise" out of Hannes, though Hannes, as a rule, was quite equal to the occasion.

121

We were bound once more for the interior, and expected to get well up towards the lakes of Arnarvatnsheithi, to visit the Caves at Surtshellir, and to see the western side of Lang Jökull, where we should again enter the uninhabited desert. The greater portion of our journey, though, would be among the western farms, in country rich in folk-lore and made famous in the Sagas.

Our way lay for several miles along the Thingvellir road, then we turned off to the left and skirted the fjord for a mile or two, soon, however, striking inland away from the coast. We passed at the foot of Lagafell, a rather striking mountain having an abrupt escarpment, and proceeded thence through grassy country to Mosfell. Soon after getting clear of Reykjavik we were met by one of our old guides, Thorlakur, who accompanied us to Mosfell, where he possessed a farm, which lay on the hillside overlooking a green plain well besprinkled with cotton grass. After lunch we went up to Thorlakur's farm, and made the acquaintance of his wife and two little girls, who entertained us to coffee. I took two photographs of the family : one showing the dwelling—a typical western farm-house of the better class—and the other with Thorlakur on his pony, and showing a tuff-capped and protected hill in the background. The grass on this farm was very thick, and in the plain below the cotton grass was so abundant that it looked as if a number of white sheets had been spread over the green.

After taking leave of Thorlakur and his family, we proceeded on our way, making a gradual ascent until reaching a spot overlooking a stream, beyond which there were some peculiarly-shaped brownish hills that presented a somewhat castellated appearance—from the distance it was difficult to judge whether they were volcanic necks, or liparite or tuff formations. On the way the weather, which had been quite fine to the time of our arrival at Mosfell, gradually changed : we could see the moisture condensing on

THORLAKUR AND HIS WIFE AND CHILDREN AT HIS FARM-HOUSE.

the mountains away to our left and straight ahead, and were much struck with the peculiar way in which the mists hung over the hills and left a valley quite clear. From the spot overlooking the stream just mentioned, we descended into the valley and crossed the river, the Leiruvogsá ; then we commenced the ascent of a long, steep track up the hillsides, between Skalafell on the east and the great mass of the mountain Esja on the west, towards the pass known

as Svinaskarth. Beyond the river, we entered the
region where the moisture was rapidly condensing,
and made our way up the path in a perfect deluge of
rain. We passed hundreds of small streams and
rivulets that came down the mountain sides across
our path. We did not mind the rain, for we were
clad in oilskins, and the weather was not cold—there
was a great difference in temperature from that of the
interior and between the ice-fields : it seemed milder,
as indeed it was, and the rain did not strike so cold.
We were experiencing the difference due to the
warmer winds from the south and south-west, and to
the effect of the North Atlantic Drift, a continuation
of the Gulf Stream. One peak of Esja to the left
was a sharp-pointed brown cone of liparite, and it
stood out as a prominent feature as we ascended.
The pass was very steep in places, and had a number
of abrupt turns in it, and there were many views that
would have made fine pictures for the camera in
clearer weather. Descending the pass into the valley
of the Sviná (Svinadal) the gradient was rather
severe, so we dismounted and led our ponies down the
steepest parts to relieve them from our weight for
a while. A very noticeable feature in Svinadal was
the number of streams that emerged from the
mountain sides, from beneath the lava flows, and then
ran down in a series of cascades to join the river
Sviná in the valley. We followed this river to
its confluence with the Laxá, which flows for a short
distance through a quantity of out-cropping lava,
roches moutonnées again, whose rounded and smoothed
surfaces stand as evidence that ice once filled the
valley. Thence we proceeded along the valley of the

Laxá (Laxadal) beside the river and through a quantity of moraine matter to Reynivellir, passing the volcanic cone of Sandfell to the right. Along the sides of this valley the straight lines of the lava flows can be traced for miles dipping but very slightly inland from the fjord (Laxavogr), which we were then in sight of.

We arrived at Reynivellir on Saturday evening and stayed there till Monday. The weather was not good, and excepting on Sunday evening, when there was a break that caused some very fine cloud-effects, it rained almost incessantly. Our first camp was made here, but as through a misunderstanding only one tent had been brought, which Miss Hastie used, the rest of the party had to make shift in another way. I elected to use the church as my place of residence, and had my bed rigged up in the loft or gallery; this loft was a veritable storehouse, so out of curiosity I made a rough inventory of the articles I found. Besides several boxes and sea-chests, there was hanging from a number of hooks a wardrobe that would have clothed about half-a-dozen persons of both sexes; then there were some large lockers, ranged along the side of the loft, that were filled with wool; a number of agricultural implements, a rocking arm-chair, and two forms completed the list.

The Icelanders are very hospitable, and travellers are made welcome. Every farmer who can afford it has one or two guest-chambers that are placed at the disposal of any one passing through. On arrival at the farm the traveller is invited to partake of coffee. When this is served in the best room of the house, the farmer and his wife join the new arrivals in a light meal, consisting of excellent coffee, and fancy pastry of equally excellent quality. Some of the Icelandic women are very good pastry-cooks, and the cakes and pastry they produce often equal in quality any that could be procured at a first-class London confectioner's.

At Reynivellir there are a farm-house and a church. The churches are either Athalkirkja (principal church) or Annexia (farmers' church), and that at Reynivellir is Athalkirkja. The clergy are appointed and paid by the Government; but they have farms which add to their incomes. The religion of the Icelanders is Lutheran. Service was held in the church at Reynivellir on the Sunday morning while we were there, and all the members of our party attended it. The minister was attired in black robes, which he wore with a white ruff and flattened hat; he looked exactly as if he had just stepped out of a Velasquez picture, for his face and dress were quite typical. It is a peculiarity of the Icelandic services that the members of the congregation come and go just as they please; evidently they consider the service of too long duration, for many leave the church and absent themselves for periods varying up to fifteen minutes. I inquired why, and was informed that the Icelanders, being used to open-air life, could not remain still and cooped up for any length of time, so they left while the service was in progress, in order to stretch their legs and occasionally to have a smoke. They were quite regardless of the time of commencement of the service, and came in at any time during its progress. The sexes did not seem to mix, for the men were seated, most of them, in the chancel around the pulpit, while the body of the church was occupied by the women, though a few men sat in the seats right at the back.

The rain continued to the time of our departure from Reynivellir, for we set out on Monday in a depressing drizzle. We had a very stiff climb by a zigzag path up the side of the Reynivallahals mountain, a flat-topped range having the valley of the Laxá on one side and the waters of Hvalfjord on the other. After crossing the highest part of the ridge, we gradually descended to the water of Hvalfjord, passing Fossá, where there is a small waterfall in a ravine, close by a wooden bridge that spans it. There was a good view from Fossá over Hvalfjord and to the head of one branch of it. To this branch we descended by a long slope on the steep mountain side, and then passed round the head of the arm, where the Brgnjudalsá runs into it over a ledge of basalt. We could not help being struck with the two bold scarped ends of the mountain ranges that come down to the fjord: Muláfjall between the two branches, and Thyrill beyond. After crossing the Brgnjudalsá, we rounded the first headland, and proceeded for some distance along the second arm of the fjord till we came to a black sandy beach, which was then covered with about six inches of water. This was fully a mile from the head of the fjord, but we crossed at this point, the ponies splashing through the water as if they enjoyed that part of the journey —and doubtless they did. Our way then lay at the foot of the great escarpment of the Thyrill mountains, a range that has been carved by the weather into wondrous fantastic shapes, the end presenting a

magnificent castellated appearance—a fine solid block
resting on a sloping base.

One of the Sagas relates how the Thyrill family
some nine hundred years ago resided on the small
island of Geirsholmi, which was probably much bigger
than it is at the present time. They had a feud with
another family, who invaded the island; but the

THE THYRILL MOUNTAINS.

Thyrills had received warning of the approach of
the enemy, and they escaped to the peninsula of
Thyrillsnes, where a sanguinary battle was fought.
All the Thyrills were slain except one woman who
had been left on the island, and she escaped by
swimming to the mainland with her baby son; she
then ascended the castellated end of the Thyrill
mountains and escaped through the gap between the
two blocks into which it is divided. It is said that

when the son grew up, he wreaked vengeance upon the family that had almost exterminated his own.

From Thyrill we proceeded along the shore of Hvalfjord for two or three miles, and on looking back, the end of the Thyrill mountains presented a remarkably fine appearance. From a base of lava and tuff, with a talus slope above, there rose the main castellated block composed of upright columns of basalt. Looking the other way towards the sea, the block of mountains known as Akrafjall, round which the fjord bends, stands as a striking feature in the landscape.

On leaving the coast we climbed some liparite and tuff rises, and then passed over a range of hills (Ferstikluhals) northward. From the divide we had a very good view over the country ahead; in a valley below there were three lakes having an outlet for their water through Svinadal, by the river Laxá, into a small fjord named Leirárvogar—this must not be confounded with the Laxá already mentioned. It should be noted that the same name is often applied to more than one mountain, river, or town, and confusion as to the geographical position may arise unless it is clearly understood which of those bearing the same name is indicated; for instance, Mosfell (mossy mountain) is applied to several mountains, Hvitá (white river) to several rivers, and Stathr. (a homestead) to several villages or farmhouses of note. We skirted two of the lakes in the valley and then passed between the last two, where Hannes made a deal in trout with a man who was fishing in a stream connecting the two lakes. We made our way through rain, which had just

K

recommenced after a fairly fine interval lasting during
most of the day's journey, to the head of the third
lake, where we found quarters for the night at the
farm-house of Draghals. Miss Hastie occupied her
tent as usual; but I, not liking the guest-chamber
because it was absolutely devoid of ventilation,—the
windows were fixed in their frames and could not be

MISS HASTIE TROUT-FISHING.

opened,—took up my quarters in a drying-shed,
a large and airy enclosure running along two sides
of the house, which was a fair-sized galvanised iron
structure. Beside this modern excrescence there stood
the old wooden-fronted, turf-walled, and grass-roofed
buildings that were formerly used as the dwelling-
house, but were then converted into kitchen and
dairy buildings—ancient and modern were side by
side.

There were some pretty scenes on the river Draghalsá, an interesting stream having a number of hard and soft dykes cut through by the water that descends in a series of waterfalls to a pool, the overflow from which runs into the lake close by. Both pool and stream afford sport for fishermen, and Miss Hastie and Jón got quite a good basket of trout there. I was less fortunate; but as I did not commence until the others had finished, I concluded

TYPICAL ICELANDIC FARMERS.

that they had caught all the fish in the stream and had left none for me to catch—but I am not a fisherman, so lack of skill may have had something to do with the small success met with.

The people here were typical Icelandic farmers, and the photographs I took give a very good idea of them. They are not altogether devoid of humour, and enjoyed my photographing our "guide, philosopher, and friend," whom I caught sharpening a knife at a grindstone. He was quite unconscious that I was

immortalising him, but the onlooking Icelanders
grasped the point of the situation, and their apprecia-
tion of it was expressed in their faces, which were
turned towards me as I took a snapshot at the group.

On leaving Draghals late in the afternoon we
climbed the hills to the north and came in sight of
a fine sheet of water about ten miles long. This is
Skorradalsvatn; it is not very broad, being less than
two miles at its widest part. Just after passing the
divide we came upon a fine waterfall at a spot where
the waters of one of the mountain streams fall a
sheer hundred feet into a deep pool below. There
are two very fine gorges here, and they join at the
confluence of two streams that then flow by a
meandering course to the lake. The delta of this
river has spread half-way across the lake, where the
width is gradually narrowing; in course of time it
will extend right across, and cut the water into two
portions. We then skirted the lake to its head,
rounding it just where it narrows to a river, which
flows on as the Audakilsá towards Borgarfjord. Just
beyond the river we came to the farm-house of Grund,
where we took up our quarters.

We remained at Grund a whole day in order that
the fishermen might again try their skill with the
rod, and they were successful in catching a number
of trout. It rained heavily during the afternoon,
which was very annoying, for it prevented me from
going to explore the mountains of Skarthsheithi and
the vicinity—a pity, for the group looks a most interesting one. Facing Grund they form a sort of
semicircle, a vast corrie having a yellowish-brown
hill in the middle, a liparite mound; to the left of

the semicircle there is another brownish mountain that is evidently a series of alternations of tuff and liparite. On the face of the mountains in the centre there are two small glaciers, while to the right there is a remarkable stepped pyramid that shows most distinctly the lava flows—flow above flow being lined out and stepped in the profile, the parallel lines being distinctly marked not only on the pyramid but also round the semicircle.

At Grund we lost our "guide, philosopher, and friend," whose engagements required his presence in Reykjavik in the course of the next few days. In the early morning he departed, and thenceforth we had to look to Hannes for guidance. Two or three hours after his departure we set out for Reykholt. Our way lay over some rough rising lava flows at the back of the farm-house, and these we ascended to the divide, whence we had a fine view of the valley of the Hvitá. It was fertile-looking country, but the land is not cultivated; grass is the only thing grown, for the sun has not sufficient strength to ripen grain of any kind. Haymaking was in full swing just then, and we saw the hay-makers at work on all the farms as we passed by. Beyond the Hvitá valley a long range of mountains stretches from near the sea far inland, the most prominent in the chain being a conical peak (Baula) some fifteen to twenty miles distant.

After crossing the river Grimsá we entered a stretch of country composed of many alluvial river terraces. Terrace above terrace had been formed in succession by the Hvitá and several of its branches that we crossed in the course of the day, namely, the

Grimsá, the Flokadalsá, the Reykjadalsá, and others. Between the two last named rivers we had lunch beside the farm-house of Kropprmuli. From the Reykjadálsá we proceeded to some hot springs, Tunguhver, close beside the river. These springs emerge from the side of a small hillock, where they bubble and boil over, and spurt jets a few feet into the air; the water comes down the hillside in a series of small waterfalls or cascades. Great volumes of steam rose from the springs, and unfortunately the wind was blowing it in such a way as to obscure the whole of the springs, except for an occasional glimpse when the steam was swirled aside by a strong gust. At one end of the hill, however, where the springs were very active, the steam was partly blown away from us, and we saw several of them in violent ebullition. On leaving this spot we made our way up the valley of the Reykjadalsá, a river that we crossed nine times in less than the same number of miles. At a spot close by one of our crossings there was, in the middle of the river, a small mound that is often the scene of eruptive violence; it was the site of the geyser, Arhver, which plays at intervals of several days—weeks sometimes, throwing a small stream of water high into the air, sometimes twenty feet or more.

At Reykholt, where we put up for the night, there are a church, parsonage, and farm. The minister was at home, and he came out to receive us as we clattered into the space in front of the parsonage. He was a big, broad-shouldered man, as broad in mind as in person, and capable of regarding things in a large way. He welcomed us in courtly fashion, and as he spoke good English we at once got on excellent terms with him. An invitation to coffee was of course accepted, and we were entertained by the minister and his wife, a woman in striking contrast to our host in point of size, for she was quite small and slim.

The Reykholt parsonage is on the site of the house of Snorri Sturluson, the historian, who lived nearly seven hundred years ago. Just below the house, and less than a hundred yards distant from it, there is a hot spring known as Skriflir, which seems to have been in existence in Snorri's time, for rather nearer to the house there is a bath that is said to have been constructed by him. It is connected to the spring by an aqueduct, also ascribed to Snorri. The water on issuing from the spring is boiling, and when it reaches the bath it has lost but little of its original heat, consequently it is impossible to bathe at once. When any one requires a tub, the water is run into it from the spring over-night, then in the morning the temperature is just delightfully warm. This bath was built in twelve hundred and something; and as Snorri died in 1241, it is not much short of seven hundred years old. A large iron cauldron that stood just close to the spring served as the laundry, for the family washing was done there. Hot springs are often utilised in this way. At Reykjavik, the capital, the whole of the washing of the town is done at a hot spring, the Laug, just outside the town, and daily numbers of women are to be seen going and returning with their wooden wash-tubs on their backs.

The Reykholt church was the largest that we had

seen away from the towns. The minister informed me that sometimes he had as many as two hundred persons in his congregation, the number varying between that and one hundred. His parish was a large one, there being thirty-five farms included in it. The parsonage was one of the prettiest imaginable, for its grassy roofs and sides were covered with a profusion of camomile flowers. I took photographs of front and back, but they give only a faint idea of the original, devoid as they are of colour.

In the valley of the Reykjadalsá just below Reykholt there is a very thick growth of peat; down by the river it was laid bare for a thickness of more than twelve feet, the thickest seam I saw in Iceland.

CHAPTER XII

THE sun had crossed the meridian next day before we left Reykholt. We had coffee with the minister and his wife, from whom we parted on the best possible terms; they and their children waved their adieux to us as we proceeded on our way up Reykholtsdal. We struck across towards the Hvitá, and soon came in sight of that river, a swift-flowing stream whose milky-white colour denoted that its source must be up in the snow- and ice-fields of the Jökulls. Along the Hvitá (white river) valley there were many evidences that the river had at one time been far wider, for up the valley sides several terraces marked levels at which alluvium had formerly been deposited. We lunched at Stori Ás, in view of the conical peaked mountain, Strutr, and Eyriks Jökull. We were then not far from the bridge that spans the Hvitá and affords communication between opposite sides of the river, so Miss Hastie and I walked on while Hannes and Jón were adjusting pack-saddles, etc. I came upon an interesting specimen of wind erosion at the top of a rise, where the sandy soil had been blown away from round a turf-covered mound. We passed

through a small birch wood, but the trees were very
diminutive, three to five feet being the average, with
a few rather more; a photograph I took gives the
impression of much greater height. On the opposite
side of the river we could see recent lava, and on the
hillside beyond, the farm-house of Gilsbakki. This
lava had come from a considerable distance, for I

A FOREST NEAR BARNAFOSS.

traced its course from Gilsbakki, right away past the
liparite mountain, Tunga, and beyond Strutr, where
it divides and flows in two streams. This lava
determines the courses of the principal rivers thereabouts, which flow along its edges.

Just below the bridge a very remarkable sight is
to be seen. For more than half a mile along the
right bank of the river a series of cascades and waterfalls flow into it. The water issues from beneath the

lava of which the steep bank is composed, and then flows down its side; it is a very striking proof of the great extent of some of the subterranean rivers. Just above the bridge there is a very fine fall in the Hvitá, known as Barnafoss; though fine, it cannot be compared with Gullfoss in grandeur, and the glory of this part of the river is the series of cascades on its right

THE CASCADES AT BARNAFOSS.

bank. The spot is supposed to have been named from the drowning of two children near the fall—Barnafoss, the children's waterfall; but the minister at Reykholt declared that the tale is not true, and that the name is more likely to have been corrupted from Bjarni, which is a man's name. It is worthy of note that the birch woods seem to flourish best in the decaying lava in the scoriaceous lava-fields; it also seems to do well in soil produced from liparite, for it grows high up on the east side of the liparite mountain, Tunga.

At the Hvitá bridge the party split into two—Miss Hastie going on with Hannes to Gilsbakki, while Jón and I went along the left bank of the Hvitá past Husafell, thence onward across the river Kaldá, where we got among lava and birches. The birches were much of the same height as those in the Barnafoss wood, though I saw several that stood about seven to eight feet high. I took a photograph of one of them—one in which the wood had attained a thickness of some three or four inches; it was the finest specimen of a birch-tree that I saw in Iceland. There are bigger birches in the land, for I have seen a photograph of a clump of about a dozen that are over twenty feet in height, but they are in a particularly favoured spot on the eastern side of the island. I got Jón on his pony to stand while I photographed the wood through which we were passing, for it was a typical Icelandic forest. On crossing the next river, the Geitá, I found the lava much broken up and denuded, and there was spread over it a quantity of the alluvial pebbles that are brought down in times of heavy rains and melting ice by the rivers flowing from Lang Jökull—it is a sort of flood plain, in fact. This continued until we reached the Hvitá, but on the other side of it we once more found ourselves upon the unbroken rough lava. Close beside this river we came to a halt for the night at the farm-house of Kalmanstunga, which is situated in a very picturesque spot facing Lang Jökull, the glaciers and ice-fields of which are in full view; it has the liparite mountain, Tunga, and a portion of Eyriks Jökull on the right, and the extinct volcano, Strutr, on the left.

In the morning I ascended the rising ground at the back of Kalmanstunga, and thence obtained an interesting view over the country. In the foreground beneath Lang Jökull a long valley filled with lava from beyond Strutr stretches away from left to right; two rivers flow down the valley, one on each side of the lava, which determines their course along its edges. The Hvitá flowed on the edge of the lava just at the foot of the hills whereon I stood; on the far side of the valley, on the other edge of the lava, the Geitá flowed at the foot of the outlying hills of Lang Jökull. Away to the right in the valley between the two rivers, towards their confluence, I could see the denuded alluvium-covered lava noticed on the way. This alluvial matter is deposited during floods, when the waters of the swollen rivers unite and flow over the lava as one.

It was nearly mid-day before we got a start, for there had been delay over a very important matter. Jón had awakened me several hours earlier to inform me that there were no candles in the house! Now, candles would not seem to be a matter of much importance to us, considering that it was then broad daylight and that we had but little use for candles in the ordinary way, because daylight continued practically during the whole twenty-four hours; nor would the lack of them seem to be a thing to cause a delay in starting; but it was really the case, for we were about to proceed to the Surtshellir Caves, and candles were required to enable us to explore their passages. That being so, a messenger had to

be sent to the farm-house at Husafell, where a stock
was generally kept for anybody wanting to visit the
caves. The caves were distant about two hours' ride
—one rarely mentions distance in the ordinary way
when travelling in Iceland, because ten miles, say,
might represent a journey of three or four hours, or
the same distance might be traversed in little more
than an hour in very favourable ground. After
crossing the rise at the back of Kalmanstunga, we
descended into the valley of the Northingafljot, a
clear-water river having its source in a number of
lakes of glacial origin known as Fiskivötn, lying
beyond Eyriks Jökull. The valley is filled with lava
from the same source as that on the Hvitá side of
Strutr, whence I had just come. Here the lava is
noted for the number and extent of the caves that
underlie it. There is a sharp rise as the river is
ascended, the stream in consequence being a swift
one—so swift, indeed, that it has been able to carve
a way through the lava, which it crosses from one
side of the valley to the other, a very unusual thing.
The upper portion flows on the western edge of the
lava and at the foot of the hills on that side; while
the lower, after crossing the lava, flows along by
the eastern edge at the foot of the mountains Strutr
and Tunga.

The caves at Surtshellir are remarkable for several
things. Their origin is probably due to a big bubble
formation, helped partly, perhaps, by a crust of lava
being forced upward in the form of an arch by
pressure acting from the sides; though there is
no doubt that they have been much enlarged and
deepened by the eroding action of flowing water.

An underground river used to flow through the caves, but as it does not do so now, some lower channel has doubtless been found. There was evidence of lower caves beneath those visited, for on stamping on the ground in several places, distinctly hollow sounds were produced. The falls into the Hvitá at Barnafoss, which are only a few miles away,

THE NORTHINGAFLJOT CUTTING ACROSS THE LAVA.

lie in the Surtshellir line of drainage, and are proof that very large quantities of water are still flowing underground in this neighbourhood; in fact, it is highly probable that a great deal of water from the numerous lakes, the Fiskivötn, on Arnarvatnsheithi, escapes underground. There are two entrances to the caves—one near what is known as the Bone Cave, the other close by the Icicle Cave. The caves are in a picturesque spot, and beyond the entrance that

we used there lies the great ice-covered Eyriks Jökull,
one of the highest mountains in Iceland.   There is
a depression in the lava at this spot—a double
depression, in fact, for inner and outer rims indicate
them very distinctly, and it is obvious that the
opening in the caves is due to the falling in of part
of the roof.   Access to the caves is obtained by

THE DOUBLE DEPRESSION IN THE LAVA AT THE ENTRANCE TO THE
SURTSHELLIR CAVES.

scrambling down the loose broken lava to an opening
at the bottom.   The photographs do not give much
idea of the roughness of the "going"; from end to
end, except in the Icicle Cave, where difficulties of
another kind were met with, the floor of the caves
was strewn with broken lava.   The fragments that
have become detached from the roof and now lie
upon the floor are angular blocks of extreme ragged-

ness and hardness, piled up in confused heaps that
test quality of boots, strength of ankles, and tough-
ness (or tenderness) of skin, to say nothing of the
mysterious capability of hanging on " by one's eye-
lids" that is almost absolutely necessary in places.

Jón and I were accompanied by the farmer from

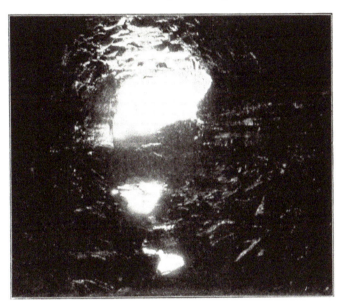

IN THE SURTSHELLIR CAVES NEAR THE ENTRANCE, SHOWING THE
WATER-WORN LINES.

Kalmanstunga, a man acquainted with the caves,
who had come with us in the capacity of guide. We
scrambled down to the entrance and then lighted our
candles. When once inside, there could be no doubt
as to one of the causes of their existence or enlarge-
ment, for there along the sides of the caves, indicating
the different levels of the old river, were numerous
water-worn lines. The photograph shows this very

L

clearly; it also shows the lava fragment bestrewn floor, and the roof from which the fragments have fallen. We followed our guide into the main channel, but he soon turned to the left into a branch known as the Bone Cave, because of the number of animal remains (bones) that bestrew the floor. It is said that some twenty to thirty outlaws at one time occupied the cave, and that the bones are the remains of the sheep and oxen which the outlaws stole from the flocks and herds in the neighbourhood, and which they consumed for food. That may have been so, or it may not, but it would account for the presence of the bones; except for some such tale it would be difficult to do so, for the animals could hardly have strayed so far from daylight, to say nothing of the difference of level between the floor of the main channel and that of the Bone Cave. This branch cave was soon explored, for in about two hundred yards the roof gradually converged to meet the floor, and we found it necessary to crawl on hands and knees—a painful thing to do over the rough angular lava blocks. Retracing our steps we descended to the old river-bed again and scrambled over rough boulders for a considerable distance, to emerge after awhile by a long rising snow slope into the open air. The snow remains in the caves all the year round; it drifts in through the opening during the winter, and the warmth of the whole summer's sun does not suffice to melt it—it was then the end of July.

The opening has been caused by the falling in of the roof, but there is no way out—the edges overhang quite beyond reach. On again we went, down another snow slope to the second section of the caves, where the " going " was indescribable. Our way lay over the roughest and sharpest-edged blocks of lava that it is possible to imagine, where nothing but the strongest of boots would have withstood the wear and tear ; it was one continuous scramble on hands and feet. I found it most difficult, for in addition to the candle in my hands, a camera was slung from my shoulders, and the wretched thing would continually work round in front and get mixed up with arms or legs at critical moments when my body was contorted in scrambling up, down, or over, a particularly awkward series of sharp-edged boulders. At last we reached another long snow slope, at the top of which there was another opening to the caves—the second entrance already mentioned. The snow-drifts are not very deep in places, for I went through twice, though I was able to scramble out again without assistance.

The last section of the caves is most remarkable. After descending into it by another snow-drift, we found ourselves in a region of frost and ice. Water trickled everywhere from the roof, crystallising into long icicles, and the drops that fell upon the floor were converted into smooth ice, or gradually built up ice stalagmites. For several hundred yards the whole floor was coated with ice ; there were myriads of icicles pendent from the roof, and on the floor stood ice stalagmites, pillars and columns innumerable. One of the first features to notice was a fine group of clear ice columns, while we came upon the most beautiful thing in the caves a little farther on, after descending an ice slope that was most difficult to negotiate without alpenstock and ice nails in boots.

However, by the exercise of great care we got down
without tumbles, and were rewarded by the sight of
a very beautiful snow-white cascade of ice; the scene
was very pretty and fairy-like, illumined as it was by
the light shed upon the surroundings by our candles.
It was after passing the cascade that the real difficulty
of the journey began. For several hundred yards we
had to make our way over countless lava boulders,
but no longer were they sharp and angular, and rough
to the touch; no, they were far otherwise, for they
were coated with ice and were as smooth as glass, and
oh, so cold! and as slippery as the proverbial glass,
only more so, for no glass could be so slippery. Up
and down we went at the slowest possible rate of
progression, climbing over huge blocks of ice-coated
lava, hanging on with hands to some of the ice
stalagmites that, fortunately for our safety, were in
hundreds—nay, thousands, and feeling cautiously
with feet for projecting pieces of ice on which to rest
them and get a sort of foothold; but our slips were
many in the pitchy darkness that was but faintly
relieved by the dull light from the candles we carried,
which we clasped convulsively in our hands as we
clutched at the icy stalagmites, and slid and slipped
and blundered along. At last we emerged from the
ice-bound region to find ourselves on scoriaceous lava,
coated in places with a thin layer of a loamy deposit.
Over this we crunched for a few hundred yards till we
came to a cairn built in the middle of the cave. In
a recess of the cairn there was a tin box, which the
guide soon brought to our notice. It contained a
number of visiting cards that had been left from time
to time by tourists wishing to immortalise themselves,

for this is one of the least visited of the "lions" of
Iceland.   On the top of the cairn, which stood nearly
shoulder high, there was a wooden board, having on
it a number of coins, ancient as well as modern, for
one of them, a Danish coin, bears the date 1743.   It
is a time-honoured custom for visitors to leave a coin
there; but as water drops from the roof upon the
board containing the coins, they speedily decompose;
indeed, many of them were already unrecognisable
from decay.   The end of the cave was but a short
distance beyond, perhaps a hundred yards, and there
two staves, about three feet long, with hollow ends,
rested in an upright position on the floor at a spot
where the roof and floor rapidly converged; they
were kept in place by the sloping roof, which meets
the floor a few yards beyond.   In the hollows of the
staves there were several old coins, one of them being
a Danish piece about the size of an English crown.
To get out of the caves we had to retrace our steps
over the ice-covered boulders and through the Icicle
Cave to the second entrance.   The photograph shows
the view looking towards the entrance just before
ascending the snow slope; we had already passed
most of the icicles, but on the floor, which is of ice,
a few of the very small stalagmites are shown.

In the Icicle Cave we met Miss Hastie and Hannes,
who had come over from Gilsbakki because the day
was so fine and summer-like—it was one of the few
days that really felt summery.   After lunch beside
the Northingafljot we started for Gilsbakki, proceeding down the lava in the Northingafljot valley.   We
crossed the river at a convenient ford not far away
and rode along on the right side of the valley.   We

passed by the liparite mountain, Tunga, this time on
the western side of it ; the lower slopes were covered
with birch, though it did not grow so far up as on
the eastern side.   The colouring of the bare exposed
rock was brown, yellow, purple, etc.—just the same
as that at the hot springs at Kerlingarfjöll, and it
looked as if several places were the sites of hot

SURTSHELLIR—THE ICICLE CAVE.

springs, then extinct.   I had no time to examine the
mountain, but I should doubtless have found the
matter quite hard, whereas that by the hot springs at
Kerlingarfjöll was of the consistency of soft clay.
Beyond Tunga, the Northingafljot lava joins that
coming from the other side of the mountain in the
Hvitá valley, and thence they continue as one flow
down the Hvitá valley to just beyond Gilsbakki.

We travelled for several miles beside the river Thorvaldsdalsá, and could not help noticing that it decreased in volume as we descended, although several streams flowed into it from the mountain-sides; its waters drain underground, and doubtless contribute to the falls on the right bank of the Hvitá, a few miles distant at Barnafoss.

CHAPTER XIII

ARRIVED at Gilsbakki I took up my quarters in the church, for the house was then rather full: besides the minister and his wife, and family of five sons and three daughters, the haymakers had to be accommodated, the total number sleeping there being twenty-six. In looking at the outside of the house, it was difficult to believe that so many persons could be stowed away there. Haymaking was in full swing on the farm, and the haymakers worked far into the night—I could hear them laughing and talking at intervals through the open door of the church, for they were in the fields all around. As there was bad weather impending, and the next day would be Sunday, they probably worked till the whole of the hay had been raked into small stacks in readiness for the rain, which fell, as expected, during most of the following day. It is noteworthy that we escaped much of the discomfort of travelling in bad weather by our Sunday rests, for it rained continuously nearly every Sunday we were in Iceland.

Though it poured nearly the whole day, there was an interval in the evening when it became a mere

drizzle, so Miss Hastie and I again visited the
Barnafoss Falls. I took several photographs thereabouts, for I saw many interesting features. At the
falls the river has several times changed its course in
eroding first one soft spot, then another. A hard
dyke stretches half-way across the gorge, and there is
a series of terraces in the old course of the Hvitá,

A LAVA ARCH.

where the river had formerly flowed, foaming and
tumbling over great steps in the rock. The gaps in
the upper terrace are clearly seen, and a little water
still flows through some of them; but the main
volume now escapes through a great gap where the
water has carved its way down to a lower level
through softer rock. There are some interesting
formations in the lava on the banks of the Hvitá,
one being an arch illustrating the origin of some of

the caves; it is obvious that this arch is due to
pressure acting from the sides, which has forced the
crust of lava upwards. This on a large scale might
have been the origin of the Surtshellir Caves, which
were subsequently enlarged by the action of flowing
water, though their origin was probably due to bubble
formation. There were also some exceedingly good

ROPY LAVA AT BARNAFOSS.

specimens of "ropy" lava, so named because of the
ropy appearance and rope-like structure of the
surface.

On leaving Gilsbakki we proceeded down the
valley of the Hvitá for a considerable distance on the
right side of the river, where there are indications,
which are quite as plain as those we saw on the other
side, that the river was at one time very much
wider, for there is much alluvial material, forming

a series of river terraces one above another, and these are intersected by various streams from the mountains.

While lunching at Sithumuli we saw great clouds of steam rising from the valley of the Reykjadalsá. A mountain range separates the valleys of the Reykjadalsá and the Hvitá where we were, but we could just see into the former round the end of the spur of the range. The steam arose from the geysers at Tunguhver, which were in great agitation and violent eruption; but we could not get across to see them, for the Hvitá intervened, and there was but one way—that over the bridge at Barnafoss, several hours distant. The track diverged from the Hvitá at Sithumuli, and our way lay over a ridge of basalt and across a series of scarped rises to the valley of the Kjarrá, a river that lower down towards its. confluence with the Hvitá is known as the Thverá. The river is bridged at Northtunga by a small iron suspension bridge. A feature in the landscape hereabouts is the conical peak of Baula; there is also a smaller peak known as Little Baula, but the former stands out prominently for many miles around. It has the appearance of a volcanic cone, but I think (I did not visit the place) the shape is entirely due to erosion; and there are many instances of this erosion, one being a peak in Arnarfjord, a photograph of which appears in its place. We had to recross the Kjarrá, and soon afterwards one of the pack-ponies took it into its head to go for a swim in the river. I laughed until I discovered that *my* box was on its back, but then my laughter was turned to concern as to the fate of the contents. I expected to find everything saturated, but was agreeably surprised, on opening it, to find that the box had proved to be almost water-tight; the damage done was practically nothing, the contents were uninjured. It was no uncommon thing for the ponies to take a swim on their own account. On another occasion one of the provision boxes was immersed, and damage to sundry articles of food resulted. We crossed the Kjarrá again, and close by came upon the tents of an Englishman who had hired the salmon-fishing for the season. No salmon-fishing was to be had in that district, as all the good rivers had been hired out.

We camped at Hjartharholt, where we managed to get eggs for our evening meal; but as egg-cups were unattainable, we had difficulty in holding the eggs in our fingers, for their temperature was near boiling-point.

Next morning I got a very good picture of the haymakers at Hjartharholt just before we set out for Statharhraun. We proceeded down the valley of the Northrá, passing, on the way to Stafholt, a number of scarped ridges of lava—these escarpments were on both sides of the river, which flowed in the depression between two of them; in the background was the conical peak of Baula, and just to the left of it a peculiar pyramidal hill formation. There are two ways from Hjartharholt to Statharhraun—one via a valley known as Vestri-Skarthsheithi, and the other, less interesting, by way of Stafholt and across the low swampy level country lying between the headlands at the end of the mountain ranges and the open sea of Faxafloi. Through a misunderstanding we started along the wrong route, and before the mistake was discovered we were well on the journey over the swamps.

A peculiar feature, common in the stony and sandy regions, must be mentioned. The surface of the ground often appears as if it had been laid out in a sort of rough design, for large stones are to be seen arranged in lines, forming irregular figures with sandy and stony matter between. The sandy waste regions in which this feature is common is known by the name *melr*, a word originally meaning " a kind of wild oat, especially bent grass, *arundo arenaria*, growing in sandy soil " ; hence the term became applied to expanses of sand, or any waste place where *melr* might grow. The explanation of these irregular figures seems to be that the earth becomes dry during the summer, and cracks under the influence of the sun's heat ; when rain falls, the particles of sand and small stones are separated from the larger lumps and drain into the cracks, leaving a network of the large stones to mark their site.

Another peculiar feature was often met with, not only in desert regions, but elsewhere. I refer to the hard-looking surfaces — apparently gravelly areas with a few stones in them—that are really a kind of bog. A pony comes to a halt on the edge of one of them, and sniffs ; its rider, a new-comer, unused to the country, urges his beast onward, but as a rule it will not go. If it does consent to move on a few paces it suddenly sinks in, and then makes a wild endeavour at recovery. After one or two experiences of this kind, the new-comer sometimes thinks it better to allow the pony to have its own way, for it seems that it knows more about the country and the nature of the ground than its rider does.

Our journey across the swamps was not devoid
of incident, for the ponies were continually sinking
into the boggy ground and performing violent
gymnastics in their endeavours to reach something
more solid. We had some compensation farther
on, for after crossing the river Langá we had to
round the headland locally named Mular, a word that
means simply a jutting crag or headland, being equi-
valent to the Scottish *Mull*. Here there are some
very fine bold scarps of basalt having a number of
hard and soft weathered dykes running through
them, the former sticking out in places like horns ;
there was a quantity of birch scrub growing on the
scree slopes (the talus) at the foot of the scarps.
Thence we went on over broken lava and through
birch scrub, past the entrance to the valley of Vestri-
Skarthsheithi and the headland of Svarfholsmuli
into the lava-filled valley of the Grjotá (Grjotardalr),
where at Statharhraun we came to a halt.

For the next day I planned a circular journey
which the local people soberly informed me would
take twenty-four hours to cover. I wanted to see
Vestri-Skarthsheithi, the valley that we had missed
by coming across the swamps to Hjartharholt, and
having formed the opinion that nothing like that
time should be required, I strongly suspected that
an endeavour was being made to " choke me off " the
journey, and therefore announced my intention of
trying whether it could be done in less time. We
set out with only a moderate food-supply, which
seemed to imply that Hannes did not consider the
journey would occupy such a long time as that
first estimated. We proceeded for some distance

along the track that we had traversed the previous
day, and rounded Svarfholsmuli, where just at the
entrance to Vestri-Skarthsheithi we pulled up at
Hraundalur to consult with the farmer as to the
route. I obtained a very good picture of Hannes
and the farmer when in consultation.

At this farm I found a woman with a dislike for

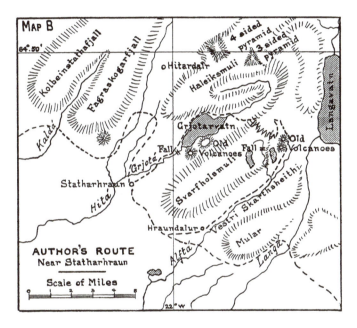

cameras ; she ran away when I happened to be
pointing mine in her direction. I took a snap-shot,
but the shutter did not work properly, so it was a
failure. Afterwards when pointing the camera in
fun at her child, who was standing beside her close
to the door of the farm-house, she mistook my intention, and snatching up the boy, ran hurriedly indoors
with him, much to my amusement. We arranged

with the farmer to come with us in the capacity
of guide; so we started off together up Vestri-
Skarthsheithi, along a track in the alluvium at the
foot of the mountains of Svarfholsmuli, where the
"going" was very good.   The valley is filled with
the lava from two volcanoes quite close to Langavatn,
a lake just beyond the head of the valley.   These are
extinct volcanoes covered with brown scoriaceous

HANNES AND THE FARMER IN CONSULTATION.

lava, and the craters are well-marked depressions,
though in each case there is a gap in the side through
which much of the lava must have flowed.   In the
lava just below there are several small vent cones,
miniature volcanoes that are quite hollow, which
spurted up small streams of lava when the locality
was a scene of eruptive activity.   From this spot we
struck up over the mountains in a north-easterly
direction, and from the high altitudes attained, got
some exceedingly fine views over a wide stretch of

country, comprising the ice-fields of Eyriks Jökull
and Lang Jökull, the mountain group of Skarthsheithi, etc.   Much nearer we looked down upon
Lake Langavatn and towards the conical peak, Baula.
On the other side we saw into the valley of the
Grjotá, in which reposed Lake Grjotarvatn, and across
to the range beyond, where very curious four-sided

SMALL VENT CONES.

and three-sided pyramids rise high above the mountain ridge.

The ponies had some very stiff work in climbing
these mountains and in scrambling down to the Grjotá
valley ; but we occasionally dismounted to give them
a rest.   Once in the valley, we were able to make
good progress beside the river to the lake, where
the shore on one side was composed of small
shingle.   The opportunity for a gallop was too good

M

to be missed, so we scampered the ponies along as hard as they could go, and they seemed to enjoy it quite as much as their riders did, for it is a rare thing to be able to gallop in Iceland. Just beyond the end of the lake we came to an extinct volcano, its truncated cone being covered with brown scoria; from this flowed the lava that now fills the valley of the Grjotá. There is no trace of lava on the lake side of the volcano, for it all flowed down towards the sea from a rift on the valley side. On we went down the valley, carefully picking our way through the lava, and travelling at a vastly different rate from that at which we had galloped beside the lake. About half a mile from Statharhraun we crossed the river Grjotá and made our way back to the farm-house, arriving there in something less than twenty-four hours from the start—to wit, within seven !

On our return there was an excellent supper ready, the result of a fishing expedition undertaken by Miss Hastie, the clergyman, and Jón. When returning, Miss Hastie's rod was broken beyond immediate repair by a collision with a pony, and it became the property of Jón, who doubtless patched it up at his leisure.

CHAPTER XIV

NEXT day, before proceeding on the direct route, Miss Hastie and I, with a local guide, made a short detour up Hitadalr. At first we picked our way through the lava, and then went on by the side of a comparatively small stream, a branch of the Grjotá. A few miles up the valley we came upon what was left of several volcanic cones, the tuff remains of which were spread over the valley. At one of these about one-third of the lip of the crater still existed, having on it a quantity of reddish scoria. The cindery tuff of these remains has weathered into very fantastic shapes. Farther up the valley the brown scoria-covered cone of a more recent volcano could be seen, but we had not time to go on, for we had to meet Jón and Hannes two or three miles beyond Statharhraun for lunch. Returning on the other side of the valley (the west), we rode along the alluvial deposits of the Hitá, a river that we crossed and recrossed several times. Near to the end of Fagraskogarfjall, a range of basalt, there is a peculiar hill, known as Gretisbali, standing away from it; this hill is a mass of cindery tuff in course of rapid

163

denudation, the result being a somewhat conical-looking hill very fantastically weather-worn. In a view that I took, the hill is on the left; to the right there is the main mass of the range, the horizontal lines of some of the basalt flows being just distinguishable. In between the basalt range and the tuff hill there is, coming down the valley, what looks (in the photograph) like a fan-shaped glacier, with a vertical face at the end, but it is merely the alluvium resulting from the denudation of the hill; the clean-cut face is due to the river Hitá, which flows very rapidly at the foot of the range, and carries away the alluvial matter as it falls over the edge of the fan. The foreground is part of a broken-up lava-field, where the vegetation is typical: birch scrub, dwarf willow, coarse grass that grows all over Iceland, mosses, etc.; they grow in the soil formed of the decomposed lava and wind-blown material filling the interstices.

Opposite the hill and at the end of the range we found Jón and Hannes awaiting us, and as lunch was ready, we had our mid-day meal before proceeding on our way. After passing the end of the Fagraskogarfjall range we crossed the river Kaldá, a stream running down to the sea from the valley between the range just mentioned and that of Kolbeinstathafjall; thence we crossed a quantity of alluvium brought down from the valley and deposited by the Kaldá in a wide belt extending from the mountains to the sea. We were making for Eldborg (fire burgh, or fortress), a "recent" volcano often referred to in the Sagas. We soon passed from the alluvium to the lava-field around Eldborg, and then

ascended by a gradual slope to the foot of the volcano,
which is a mere ring of green scoria. Up the steep
slope we scrambled to the top, and there found ourselves on the ridge of a very narrow ring of loose lava
surrounding a deep crater—a great yawning hole in
the earth below us. The lip is much serrated and
weather-worn, and the broken lava of the sides is
held together by the moss that grows in the interstices. From Eldborg we struck across a cotton-grass
swamp, and had a bad time on the way—perhaps,
however, the ponies had the worst of it, for we were
seated on their backs, sticking on for " all we were
worth," while they plunged and scrambled along,
performing a series of remarkable feats as first a hind-
leg, then a fore-leg, and sometimes two, three, or even
all four legs, sank deep down into the soft, spongy
matter of which the ground was composed. At last
we came to the river Kaldá again, and crossed to the
firmer alluvial ground, over which we cantered to the
farm-house of Kolbeinstathir, where we camped for
the night.

As usual I occupied the church, which was now
to be put to a new use. The farm-house was very
small, and there being no guest-chamber in which we
could take our meals, the church had to be requisi-
tioned to supply the accommodation it lacked. We
dined and breakfasted in it, and I took a photograph
showing the corner in which the breakfast-table was
laid. As a special mark of attention we were here
supplied with coffee flavoured with cinnamon ; now
Miss Hastie had a firmly-rooted dislike to the flavour
of cinnamon, so the attention fell flat in her case,
and I dropped in for the good things the local goddess

had sent. Jugs and basins were rather scarce, and Miss Hastie had to perform her ablutions in the porridge bowl, while the water for that purpose was brought in the coffee-pot. At this farm haymaking was completed and the hay being brought in by ponies. The bundles were hooked upon a pack-saddle, one on each side of the pony.

We had before us an interesting journey across the peninsula of Snaefellsnes from near Faxafloi, the sea south of it, to the great fjord on the north side, Breithifjord. From Kolbeinstathir to Rauthimelr we made our way chiefly over a series of swamps, where we had the usual experiences, and the ponies the usual bad times. Hannes' pony got bogged, and he was obliged to dismount in a particularly soft place. We skirted a plain of lava, or rather a series of lava flows surrounding the old volcanic cones from which they had issued; many of these were so distinct that there could be no difficulty in apportioning the lava to particular volcanoes, for the ends of some of the flows were vertical faces.

Rauthimelr lies just at the foot of the mountains, and from the farm we struck up into them, for several miles following up a branch of the Haffjathurá, a river that we had previously crossed in the plain just by the edge of the lava. After awhile we reached a spring of water—a "carbonic acid" spring it is called. The water bubbles up from the ground under cover of a shed that has been erected over it; it contains soda in solution, and is strongly impregnated with carbonic acid gas. Were this spring in a more accessible place and the property of a mineral-water manufacturer, it would no doubt bring him a considerable accession of wealth. The quality of the water is excellent, as I ascertained on taking a whisky and soda from it—that is, the soda-water came from it, the whisky being abstracted from our stock of medical comforts.   Rauthamisolkaldá is the name of the spring—I did not trouble to commit it to memory, but made a note of it !

The mountains over which we were passing were composed of a series of flows of basalt one upon another, and as usual in this formation we found many waterfalls in the course of the branch of the Haffjathurá that we continued to follow up. I took a photograph of the confluence of this branch with another (I could not ascertain their names—they did not seem to have any), and also of two of the water-falls that we saw ; there is a conical mountain in the background of one of them, but it is not a volcano— it is merely another instance of the typical weathering of a series of basalt flows.

We caught sight of many fine peaks as we ascended, but just beyond the divide they were gradually shut out as we descended into what would have been a rather dull and uninteresting valley, but that after a mile or so the river flowing there (which at first increased in volume) gradually became smaller and smaller as we descended, and this in spite of the fact that a number of mountain streams coming down on each side of the valley added their waters to it ; finally, the river disappeared altogether. I further noticed that the mountain streams had gradually been contributing less and less of their waters, and when the river was no more, the streams coming down the valley sides also disappeared before arriving

at its bottom.   There was an underground river of
considerable magnitude flowing down the valley
beneath the great accumulations of moraine pebbles
with which it was filled; as the pebbles were all of
large size they were separated by large vacant spaces,
and the thickness of the deposit must have increased
very rapidly to allow the much greater volume of
water to flow through it below the surface.   Several
miles lower down, where an area of flat land was
met with, the river reappeared, flowing on the surface of the land once more, through fine grass country
—a striking contrast to the dry valley of pebbles.

We then came in view of the sea on the north side
of Snaefell Peninsula at Alftafjord, a fjord that is
dotted over with hundreds of islands, the majority of
which are very small.   From here we made a rapid
descent to the shores of the fjord, where at Narfeyri
we camped, later in the evening witnessing a very
fine red sunset over the fjord.   My pony behaved
rather badly this day, stumbling frequently: he fell
with me twice, nearly unseating me on the second
occasion.   It is really wonderful, when the state of
the ground is considered, that the ponies do not
stumble more often; some of them rarely ever make
a mistake, others get a bit careless at times, and then
they stumble along in a free and easy sort of way,
though they rarely come a real " cropper."

Next morning Miss Hastie was amused at the
persistent staring of a small boy, who stolidly looked
at her, in spells of ten to fifteen minutes without a
blink, through the window of the guest-chamber where
we were breakfasting.   Afterwards, when I sallied
out camera in hand, the same small boy turned his

attention to me, and eyed me just as attentively
as he had Miss Hastie.   I thought that a boy who
could stare so well deserved to be immortalised, so I
brought my camera to bear upon him, with the result
that I have him in a characteristic attitude, staring
for " all he was worth " ; he was *quite* unconscious of
what I was doing, and was not posing for his photograph.   I have him in another picture, that below,

HANNES AND JÓN LOADING UP A PONY.

in which Jón and Hannes are loading up a pony, and
are hooking two of the boxes upon the pack-saddle ;
but though he was paying some attention to his
collar, he still had his weather eye on me.

I obtained an excellent view of a field of cotton
grass, in which several of our ponies were grazing,
looking across the waters of Breithifjord.   I also
caught an old woman busy stacking peat, while
smoking her pipe with evident enjoyment.

On leaving Narfeyri we skirted the foot of the

mountains at the back of the farm-house, and passed round them towards the head of Alftafjord, a name signifying swan-fjord. This is one of the places where numerous swans resort during the breeding season. We had timed our start so as to catch the tide at the ebb when nearly low water; this enabled us, by crossing the fjord some little distance from its head, to cut off more than a mile. When in the middle of the water some of the bedding broke loose and got wetted. While the packs were being adjusted, the ponies stopped for a drink of salt water, for which they have a taste, and they indulge it whenever opportunity occurs.

Our destination was Stykkisholm, whence we expected to embark in three or four days' time on board the ss. *Vesta*. After crossing the fjord we skirted it for awhile, proceeding in a northerly direction just at the foot of the mountains, which there came down close to the water's edge. We passed over a quantity of moraine material, and then entered green fertile-looking fields once more, where a number of farm-houses were dotted over an undulating tract of country. Before long we came upon a road, a *made* road leading over a series of basalt rises to Stykkisholm. When near Helgafell we made a slight divergence from the road to a farm-house, where we halted for lunch.

Afterwards we went across to Helgafell, a hill of columnar basalt rising two or three hundred feet above the surrounding low-lying land. It was curious to note that wherever the columns were broken, there on the top, where a little soil had gathered, vegetation was growing in comparative

luxuriance. From the hilltop we obtained a most
excellent view of the surroundings, comprising mountain and hill, sea and lake, a meandering river,
islands and islets. There was plenty of light and
shade and colour, sunshine and cloud, to make up
a picture; but the scene could not be done justice
to by camera, which only records physical features,
and could not reproduce effects that impressed me.
The hill is situated on a peninsula jutting into
Breithifjord; it is the site of one of the earliest of
the Christian churches built in the land. In " heathen
days the hill was sacred to the god Thor," and
before any one was permitted to look upon the holy
place, he had to perform certain rites. Helgafell and
the neighbourhood is often referred to in the Sagas.
At the foot of the hill there are now a farm-house and
a church. While passing the farm-house, one of the
Iceland dogs made demonstrations of friendship—
they are all more or less friendly—and he stood
very nicely to have his photograph taken.

From Helgafell to Stykkisholm is but a short
distance, and we covered it in less than an hour.
On the way we saw a very fine reflection of clouds
in one of the branches of the fjord where the water
was perfectly still, the beauty of the scene being due
chiefly to the colours.

CHAPTER XV

STYKKISHOLM is a very picturesque little town built in a valley and on the slopes of the enclosing hills. It is situated at the extreme end of the peninsula, overlooking Breithifjord and its branch, Hvammsfjord. In front of the town, the island of Sugandisey acts as a sort of breakwater, and affords shelter from storms to small craft. This island is composed of columnar basalt; it is a striking feature in the surrounding scenery, where hundreds of smaller islands dot the fjord.

We were put up at the house of the Rural Dean of the district, where we remained for two or three days exploring the neighbourhood until the steamer from Reykjavik called on its way to the fjords of the north-west, north and east coasts. Here at Stykkis-holm Miss Hastie and I changed about as regards sleeping apartments, for she occupied the guest-chamber in our host's house, while I camped in the tent that she had abandoned. The tent was pitched in the grounds of an adjoining house, the owners of which did not seem to mind at all, for they readily granted permission for it to be put up there.

The next day, Sunday, it rained as usual, so we did not go very far from the house.

On Monday, accompanied by our host, we set out for a mountain to the south of Helgafell, where it was rumoured specimens of coal, lignite, and gold were to be seen, but we had doubts as to what we should find. On the way I had a difference of opinion

THE COLUMNAR BASALT ISLAND, SUGANDISEY.

with my pony. He had lately developed a habit of suddenly jumping aside from all pools of water that lay in his path. I had previously not checked the growing habit, but after the previous day's rain the road was a series of puddles, so I objected to being continually switched off to right or left at the pony's sweet will, and therefore brought him up to all the puddles. At first he would not go through unless brought up to them from ten to twenty times; at last, however, he consented to do it in fewer, and at the end of the day's journey he was completely broken in. We took the road via Helgafell·to Saurar, and thence traversed a swamp, some moraine matter, and alluvium to the foot of the mountain that was our destination, Drapuhlitharfjall—a name that Miss Hastie vainly endeavoured for days to get the correct pronunciation of, and I am not at all sure that I was quite successful myself. The mountain is a mass of liparite, which is there found in all its varieties. I had strongly suspected the so-called coal to be obsidian, the black form of liparite; and on ascending the mountain to the spot where it was supposed to exist, obsidian it was found to be. Having camera in hand, I had an awkward scramble up a very steep scree slope, and I often started small avalanches, which scattered in all directions on their descent. Our host ascended by a longer and easier route: he was up before me, and crossed the scree at a higher altitude, with the result that he started an avalanche of big jagged boulders that passed perilously near to where I was lying flat upon the slope and endeavouring to wriggle upward—a yell from me caused him to wait until I had reached his level before proceeding farther.

We lunched on the mountain-side, and then went down to the supposed gold mine at its foot. On the way up we had called at a farm-house on the lower slopes of the mountain, and had there enlisted the services of the farmer to show us the shortest way up to the coal (!) and to dig out some gold. He had come provided with pick and shovel, so on reaching the mine he set to work and soon handed up a quantity of earth having a number of bright, shining, yellow metallic crystals in it, and these he pointed out as the gold. I smiled, having seen much of the same sort of thing in other parts of the world. It was iron pyrites! The mistake was not to be wondered at, for the metal had deceived many people before. I told the man that he would not get much gold out of it; but he did not seem to believe me, for he stated that a quantity of it had been sent to America, had there been tested, and had been reported on to the effect that of gold there was " a trace."

The search for gold having proved abortive, we returned to the farm-house. It was then raining hard. I wanted, before leaving the neighbourhood, to pay a visit to a lava-field some two hours distant, so I let Hannes decide whether we should go on through the rain, or make a separate journey there on the morrow. Hannes elected to go on then, because he wanted, if possible, to give *all* the ponies a rest the next day, for he was to start with them on the way back to Reykjavik the following day. We set out in torrents of rain—Hannes and I, the rest of the party remaining under shelter at the farm-house, where they were regaled with coffee, etc. I fancy they thought me a lunatic, but I was bent on seeing the lava-field of the Berserkers, where two members of that race are reported to lie buried. We started with the rain beating in our faces; the going was good, for the ground was alluvial, so Hannes led off at a hand gallop, in the evident intention of " getting through with it" as quickly as possible. I followed close at his pony's heels, and away we went through a perfect deluge of rain. It beat violently in our faces, but we did not care, enveloped in oilskins as we were; and save for my face, which was thoroughly well washed, and for a few drops of water that trickled down my neck, I rode through it all with dry skin. The rate at which we travelled brought us to the edge of the lava-field in far less than the two hours stated as necessary for the journey; in fact, we got there in about an hour and a quarter. In the last quarter of an hour the weather, as so often happens in Iceland, underwent a very rapid change: the rain ceased, the clouds condensed over the hills and finally rolled away, and by the time that we were ready to return, it was a fine clear evening.

The story connected with the Berserkers' lava-field (Berserkjahraun) is related in the Eyrbyggja Saga; it is as follows. There were two Berserkers, or Berserks, brothers named Halli and Leiknir, one of whom was anxious to obtain in marriage Ásdísa, the daughter of one Styr; but Styr had no fancy for the marriage, for he regarded him as unworthy of his daughter; yet he had not the courage to decline the match, because the Berserks were men of valour, and he did not think it safe to decline; so he was diplomatic and sought a way to circumvent them. He consulted one Snorri, a priest, with the result that Styr imposed a task upon the Berserks, that they should make a road through the lava-field within a time that he considered an impossible one, agreeing that on the successful completion of the work his daughter should be given in marriage to one of them, though which was the suitor is not mentioned in the Saga. The Berserks willingly undertook the task, for they were strong men and

had confidence in their own powers, and they set
about the work in earnest. It soon became apparent
to Styr that he had misjudged the capabilities of
the two Berserks, and that they would complete
their undertaking within the allotted time; so he
thought out a scheme and built a bath-house. When
the Berserks had finished making the road—and a
very good road it is, as the photograph shows,

THE BERSERKERS' ROAD THROUGH THE LAVA-FIELD.

certainly the best pathway that I met with in lava
—Styr invited them to take a warm bath, remarking
that they would find it very refreshing after their
arduous labours. He had prepared for their reception,
and the furnaces had been heated far beyond what
was necessary. The Berserks accepted the invitation
and entered the bath unsuspectingly. They thought
it hot, but on finding the water becoming much
hotter, they concluded that something must be

N

wrong, and their suspicion was confirmed when they discovered that the door had been barricaded against them. . They were strong men, as has been stated, and their strength was equal to the occasion, for they broke down the door. Now this contingency had been provided for : a fresh ox-hide had been spread outside the door, so when the Berserks emerged with a rush, they fell when crossing the slippery hide; one was slain as he lay sprawling on the ground, while the other was thrust back into the bath and soon became boiled Berserk. Styr afterwards went around bragging of his prowess! The pith of the story lies in the sequel, for Snorri, the priest, married Ásdisa !

In the lava, just beside the road through it, there is a mound where the Berserks are said to lie buried ; that may be so or not, but the mound was opened some time ago and human remains there found. The mound is shown in the picture of the lava-field—a small square patch just in front of the two ponies that we left standing on the pathway to indicate the spot. The Berserkjahraun farm-house lies in the middle of some hummocky land adjoining the lava-field; it is built on the site of Styr's house and named after the Berserks.

The weather was most unfavourable next day, for it rained during the greater part of it, the result being that we were confined to the house until late in the evening. However, we made an inspection of the library, where there is the nucleus of a good collection of books; it is questionable, though, whether the books will last long, for the dampness of the atmosphere is already playing havoc with them :

many that I took down from their shelves were in
a badly mildewed state, the leaves and binding being
already in an advanced stage of decomposition. The
following day we were to have embarked on board
the *Vesta*, and to have set sail from Stykkisholm.
The vessel hove in sight at about ten in the morning,
but a very strong wind was blowing—straight in
shore, too; so she remained all day under shelter of
an island a few miles out to sea, and did not come
to Stykkisholm till about eleven at night. The
weather was fine overhead during the day, so we
were able to get out a bit. I took a number of photographs, including several of the town; one showing the
sea-front was taken from a small headland a few yards
away from my tent. Our hostess kindly sat for her
photograph attired in the national costume, which
is donned on high days, holidays, and festivals. The
head-dress (*faldr* is the Icelandic name) is peculiar;
it is in shape somewhat like the French cap of
Liberty, with a horn curling over to the front, and
having a short veil which is thrown back from the
head; a gold or silver band is, as a rule, worn round
the forehead just below the cap. When wearing the
ordinary head-gear a lady's dress is not considered
complete unless an apron is worn, and it is not at
all the thing to appear in public without one. With
the *faldr* an apron is *not* necessary.

Jón and Hannes set out early in the afternoon on
the return journey to Reykjavik. I attempted to
photograph them just as they were leaving the
grounds at the back of our host's house, and again
when the pack-train was ascending the main street,
with Jón and Hannes bringing up the rear—the last

I saw of them ; but the shutter of the camera jammed, so the pictures were failures.

In the afternoon Miss Hastie went for a ride, using an Icelandic lady's saddle, but she did not go far, for she did not take kindly to it.

We took leave of our kind host and hostess after coffee next morning, and went on board the *Vesta* for breakfast. As we proceeded to the wharf, we passed some women who were carrying goods on bearers and loading up small cargo-boats for shipment by the *Vesta*.

CHAPTER XVI

THE *Vesta* set sail at about 1 P.M., shaping a course northward in Breithifjord through a sea of small islands, which I thought to be the remains of old lava flows denuded and perhaps sunk below sea-level. I had no opportunity of examining them, but they are said to be "crater islets," most of them. The sea in Breithifjord is very shallow, and on the journey to the island of Flatey, and afterwards thence towards the open ocean, our course was anything but a straight one; so shallow was the water in one place after leaving Flatey, that the wash of our vessel raised breakers on the edge of a long line of submerged bank lying parallel to and not far from our course.

Flatey is one of the remains of a broken-up lava flow; a small island opposite the town has a peculiar circular harbour whose shape is rather suggestive of a coral atoll, but perhaps this is one of the "crater islets." I did not examine it, because we had no opportunity of going ashore: we arrived just as dinner was announced, and steamed away within ten minutes of the completion of the meal. The waters of Breithifjord were alive with thousands of puffins, which flapped along the surface of the water or dived beneath it as our vessel approached. We passed through miles of them while skirting the southern coast of the North-West Peninsula. The sea was quite calm as we steamed out of the fjord and rounded the south-western corner of the peninsula, in strong contrast to the heavy winds and stormy seas of the day before. We entered Patreksfjord when it was growing dark, and came to an anchorage just at midnight.

In the early morning I turned out to look at the scenery in Patreksfjord; it was rather forbidding. We were surrounded by high mountains which came steeply down to the water's edge, there being but little land available for cultivation or for grazing purposes in consequence. I found that there would be no time to go ashore, for we were to start in half an hour's time, and there was no boat available to take me; in any case, there was nothing much but the wild surroundings to be seen, and they could be viewed just as well from the vessel's deck.

At about breakfast-time we arrived opposite to Biludalr in Arnarfjord. We were in a decidedly picturesque spot, and no doubt we were more favourably impressed because of the clear bright sky and sunny weather. Ashore, the chief interest centred in the cod-fish curing and storing station, where many women, assisted by a few men, were employed in the various branches of the industry. It was the best-equipped station that I saw in Iceland; everything seemed to be in order, and to be carried on in a thoroughly business-like way. There was a tram line running between two long rows of well-built galvanised iron sheds that lined the track.

It was in this fjord while on the way out that I obtained, on the north side, a photograph showing excellently the typical cone-like form to which a succession of basalt flows are reduced by erosion. There were other features of interest : on the south

A BASALT MOUNTAIN CONE DUE TO EROSION.

side of the fjord there were many fine specimens of corries, but the position of the sun prevented a successful attempt being made to photograph them, though, just when turning into Dyrafjord, I caught a good specimen in a suitable light. A little farther on, at Hraun, there was a view looking up a valley where the face of a moraine is kept straight by the wash of the sea at its base. We proceeded up Dyrafjord as far as Thingeyri, where we anchored.   Distant about three miles, at Framnes, there was a whale-fishing station, where whales, brought in by the whalers, were being reduced to the commercial forms of oil, bone, and manure.   We—a party of four—obtained a boat and sailed across to the station.   We were courteously received by the foreman, who kindly showed us over the factory and explained matters as we proceeded; he was a Norwegian who had been whale-fishing for seventeen years before he was appointed foreman of these works. The first thing that struck us—so severely, indeed, that we were nearly bowled over—was a very choice assortment of "smells" of the most objectionable kind: they had a distinct flavour of ancient whale, and were all more or less (generally more, and some-times most) disgusting.   We were conducted by the foreman to a platform where the whales were cut up. A dozen or more were floating in the water beyond some wooden staging that jutted out into the fjord. They are kept there until required to be cut up and placed in the boiling-down vats; then one is hauled upon the platform and cut into big slabs.   The platform was a horrible sight, covered as it was with slimy offal and refuse; this stuff, being valueless, is disposed of by being shot into the fjord, there to pollute its water.   Below the platform a similar state of things existed, and the stench that arose from the decomposing matter was too disgusting for words to describe.

The slabs of blubber are thrown into a rotary machine, where a number of knives reduce them to pieces of much smaller size; thence the blubber is taken into the boiling-down room and boiled for ten hours in great cylindrical tanks by having steam passed through. At the expiration of that time the oil has been set free and is floating on the top, whence it is drawn off into casks; it is then shipped to Glasgow to be refined. The whale-bone, which is taken from the upper jaw of the head, is cut away and piled in heaps in a yard near the cutting-up platform. The bones are sent to another room, and are there boiled; they are then dried and ground to a fine powder; this bone dust is exported in sacks for manure. The refuse of the blubber, after the extraction of the oil, is dried in special revolving machines, which reduce it to the consistency of coarse meal; this also is used as manure, and commercially is called guano. The whale-bone is taken from the heaps to the shed; it is first pulled apart and then washed in vats·containing soda and water; it is afterwards dried, when it is ready for exportation. In the blacksmith's shop we were shown the harpoons used on the whaling-vessels in securing the whales. They are shot from a short cannon into the whale; the head is hollow, and is filled with gunpowder; when the whale dashes off, the tension on the line attached to the harpoon causes the arrow-headed blades to expand and the charge of gunpowder to explode; the shell bursts and usually kills the whale. A vessel carries two harpoons, to each of which three hundred fathoms of rope is attached; the second harpoon is discharged if the first does not kill the whale. I took a photograph at Thorshavn in the Faroes showing a modern whaling-vessel. The bird's-nest where the look-out man is posted is on the fore-mast, and the harpoon gun is in the bows of the vessel. We returned to the *Vesta* with the distinct impression that we were taking along with us on boots and clothes some remnants of smelly whale, for the odour seemed to stick to us and accompany us wherever we went; it was days before all suspicion of whale wore away.

The next port of call, in Onundarfjord, was not very interesting as regards scenery. The chief industry is carried on at a large whale-fishing and boiling-down station at Flateyri, where we anchored opposite the town. The presence of the station was made evident to me as I lay in my bunk in the small hours of the morning, by the fine full-flavoured aroma that came wafting into the cabin through the open port-hole. We made but a short stay at this port, for we departed before breakfast, and were thus enabled to enjoy that meal free from the disturbing influences of whale.

We entered Skutilsfjord, a branch of Isafjord, at about mid-day, and anchored opposite the town of the same name, Isafjord. Miss Hastie and I went ashore soon afterwards and proceeded up the valley towards Flateyri, intending to walk to the ridge overlooking Onundarfjord; but the Fates, in the form of bad weather, were against us, for it rained so heavily that we abandoned our original intention after we had ascended to a considerable altitude and had become thoroughly wetted. We stood for awhile with our backs against the leeward side of a cairn on the mountain-side, trying to imagine that we had effectual shelter; but as the cairn was of rather less height than we ourselves, and as we could feel the raindrops trickling down the backs of our necks, the reality was rather at variance with our attempts at imagination. Shelter or no shelter, we stuck to our posts while devouring biscuits and cheese, and sandwiches made of Danish sausage and such like greasy delicacies, and did not abandon our post, or the intention of going to the summit of the divide, until we had finished lunch and had become uncomfortably soaked. Then we retraced our steps down the valley, by the side of a small stream that descended in a series of rapids and waterfalls. On the way we met some men road-making, and found them using a cart for conveying material for the purpose from a quarry on the roadside—the first cart that I had seen in use in Iceland. Almost opposite to our anchorage there was a good example of a small corrie high up above the water of the fjord, but the photograph proved a failure. Isafjord is reputed to be the third town in Iceland in point of population; its importance is due to the cod and herring fisheries, and to the establishments where curing is carried on. A small cod-liver oil factory emitted an odour that caused us to avoid its immediate vicinity. With regard to this oil, it has been said that some of the so-called cod-liver oil is not derived from the cod at all, but is really produced from the liver of the Greenland Shark, known locally as *hakarë* (Danish name *haukal*). I was assured, however, by one Danish merchant that this is not the case. Modern inventions were brought to mind on seeing telephone posts and the wire that connects Isafjord with Eyri. I ought to mention that one modern invention, the cream separator, is in common use on the best farms throughout Iceland. I was often awakened in the morning by hearing the whirring of the rapidly rotating cylinder of the machine. A whale-fishing establishment was said to be somewhere in the main branch of Isafjord away round the point, but we could not see it when coming in, and we were quite content not to smell it. It was doubtless several miles distant, though that avails but little when the wind blows from the direction of decaying or boiling whales.

We left Isafjord in the early morning, and between 7 and 8 A.M. rounded the northernmost point of the North-West Peninsula, known as The Horn, or North Cape. It is said to be a bold, striking headland; but as the upper portion was enveloped in fog, we could not see it properly. Fog soon afterwards descended over the sea, and the vessel slowed down to half speed; while the steam-whistle screeched out at short intervals its warning to other vessels. The result was, that we saw nothing whatever of the coast along which we were passing. It was a great pity, for that part of the peninsula, which faces northeast and is known as the Hornstrandr, is the wildest, most inhospitable, and one of the least productive regions of Iceland. There the inhabitants eke out a precarious livelihood chiefly by wild-fowling—a most dangerous occupation in that region, and it is carried on at the cost of not a few human lives; they have a very hard struggle for existence and are often on the verge of starvation. The habitations are exposed to the rigours of the weather, which are very severe, for the coast is blocked with drift ice during more than half the year, and its effect is felt for a much longer period.

In consequence of the fog we did not reach

Reykjarfjord until the afternoon was well advanced ; but at its entrance we experienced a delightful change, for we suddenly emerged from the sea fog into bright sunshine. We anchored opposite the small settlement known as Kuvikr, in a picturesque fjord where the mountains on the south side rise to a sharp-looking ridge between Reykjarfjord and Veithileysa, a fjord lying to the south. After enjoying the sunshine on deck for an hour, Miss Hastie and I went ashore and ascended the lower part of the ridge just mentioned to a sort of secondary ridge, overlooking much of the surrounding country. We found a continuation of the sea fog lying below us over Veithileysa and the valley at its head, the peaks of the mountains on the far side of the fjord standing out clear and bright in the sunshine.

A few minutes later we had an unusual experience. The fog was being blown up the fjord and over the valley at its head towards us, while the sun, which was shining brightly behind us, was rather low down in the heavens. The time was just 7 P.M. I moved away from Miss Hastie, who was sitting on a rock, to some higher ground about a hundred yards distant ; as I reached the highest point, I was astonished to see, cast upon the fog, an elongated dark shadow of myself, with an oval halo of brilliant colours around the shadow. My head was the centre of the halo, and there around it shone a bright golden yellow light ; this gradually changed in the outer rings to green, and so on through blue and indigo to violet ; then the colours of the spectrum were continued outward in the reverse order, from violet to indigo, blue, green, yellow, orange, while the outside ring was a brilliant red.　The effect was rather startling at first, as may be imagined from the sketch I made on the spot, and superstitious persons would have thought it to be a very strong omen of something or other—good or otherwise.　I was very unfortunate

A "GLORIFIED" SHADOW ON THE FOG OVER VEITHILEYSA.

in having just exposed the last film (isochromatic) in my camera, so I was unable to secure any better record than that sketched in my note-book.　It is further unfortunate that, in developing the negative I took only a few seconds before the "glorified" shadow appeared,—a view looking across the fog or clouds to the mountain peaks rising above it,—I completely

destroyed the only photographic record I had of the
scene ; for instead of pouring pyro into the solution
to hasten development, I inadvertently took up the
hypo bottle and used some of its contents, with the
result that the negative was absolutely destroyed
before I guessed what I had done—my annoyance
can be imagined, but not expressed in words ! The
appearance in the sketch was that produced while I
was drawing with arms bent and book held before
me. When I held my arms in different positions,
the shadow of course varied, but without affecting
the form or position of the oval-shaped halo. When
I had finished the sketch, I saw Miss Hastie coming
towards me, and beckoned to her to hurry, but
she arrived when the fog was clearing and the halo
fading away. I then learned that she had had
a similar experience from the spot where I had left
her seated, and that she had seen her own shadow surrounded by a halo, which accompanied her for a considerable distance as she came towards me, but faded
away as the atmospheric conditions gradually changed.

These halos are known as *Anthelia* (Greek =
" opposite the sun ") or *Glories*. The rings may be
circular if the shadow is thrown in an upright
position upon the fog, but when the shadow is
elongated through being thrown at an angle upon
it, as in my own case, they are elliptical in consequence. In all cases the observer sees the rings
round the shadow of his head, and they have a
common centre " in the point where a line from the
sun through the eye of the observer meets the fog."
I saw two brilliant *sets* of coloured rings, though more
are sometimes seen ; but those beyond are much fainter.

CHAPTER XVII

BORTHEYRI in Hrutafjord was our next port of call.
It was by no means an interesting place : the country
was low-lying, and the settlement consisted of a few
houses only. We left early in the afternoon, and
steamed almost due north out of the fjord. When
in Hunafloi beyond the promontory that separates
Hrutafjord and Mithfjord, we obtained an excellent
view, looking straight up Mithfjord, of Eyriks
Jökull. Later on, after rounding the promontory of
Vatnsnes, and when crossing Hunafjord towards
Blonduos, we caught sight of Lang Jökull, and could
trace distinctly the line of the ice-field, although
nearly seventy miles distant.

We anchored opposite Blonduos late in the
evening. The settlement consists of a store or two,
a few houses, and a church. We did not go ashore,
for no boat was available until the sun had set, and
it was getting quite dark. It was about a quarter-
past nine when the sun descended below the horizon.
The sunset effects were very fine — one of those
magnificent sights that Iceland is famous for.

The Blandá, one of Iceland's largest rivers,

discharges its waters into the fjord at Blonduos, which lies at its mouth. The river rises at Lang and Hoff Jökulls, and brings down thence considerable quantities of glacier water, proof of which is the whitish colour of the water of Hunafjord round about Blonduos. Seals were said to abound there; one was seen, I believe, but my own eyes did not fall upon it.

Skagastrond was not much more than an hour's sail. The coast hereabouts is not so precipitous as that all round the North-West Peninsula: there is more lowland between the shore and the mountains, which stand back several miles from the coast, and the nature of the country is more undulating. The original level of the lava flows of this peninsula, Hegranes, can be well seen, as we saw it, from the western side of Hunafloi. The land has been much more worn down than has that of the North-West Peninsula, and only comparatively small fragments of the upper flows remain. I went ashore in the afternoon and found the land rather swampy, with peat bogs in places. A very small boy and a dog bigger than the boy both made friendly overtures to me when I was strolling along by the beach; they were both sportively inclined, and engaged in several rough-and-tumble scrambles. There are several small islands in the vicinity whereon the eider duck has its home, and where it brings forth its young during the nesting season in the spring. The eider-duck industry is an increasing one, and year by year the birds are more cared for.

We reached Sautharkrokr early the next morning, and after breakfast I went ashore. The town is built under the steeply sloping face of an old moraine, the material of which was brought down the valley at the back of the town; a stream runs down the valley by a channel which it has eroded through the old moraine matter. From a prominent situation above the town I obtained a good view up the Herradsvötn (the left bifurcation of it, that is), where there is a lake several miles long close to the mouth of the river. The lake was no doubt at one time part of Skagafjord, and it is probable that the northerly seas rolling up the fjord met the waters of the river laden with solid particles, and caused the deposition of the detritus and the gradual formation of a bar; the final stages were doubtless the gradual widening of the alluvial dam, and the gradual filling up of one side of the lake itself. Looking up the valley I saw our old friend Maelifell-shnukr standing out prominently to the right at a distance of but twenty-five miles. In Sautharkrokr a peculiar dwelling attracted my attention; it was the deck-house of an old wrecked vessel.

One of the few wild animals found in Iceland is the blue fox; we had two on board the *Vesta*. Though in a hopeless state of captivity they were quite untamed, and snapped at any one who attempted to be friendly with them.

On leaving Sautharkrokr and sailing two or three miles north into Skagafjord, Kolbeinsdalr opened out on the east side. This valley has been fairly well worn down: there is a mass of moraine matter on the sea front, which is cut through by a mountain stream from the Unadal and Myrkar Jökulls. Farther north the valleys of Deildardalr and Unadalr came into view. Then we passed between a tuff hill that almost hides Lake Hofthavatn, and Drangey Island, where an outlying Kerling rock (old woman) stands pillar-like beside it ; there was a Karl rock (old man) also, but it fell recently. Malmey Island was next passed. The section of this island is peculiar, for a thick stratum of what looks like iron-stone lava lies on the top, then there are two or three layers of basaltic lava with what is apparently sedimentary strata between them, and beneath all there is some tuff. The situation of Lake Hofthavatn is also peculiar. The tuff hill in front of it is connected with the mainland by the merest strips on each side ; the hill was no doubt an island not long ago, and the strips of land are beaches washed up by the action of the sea on the north ·side, and on the south by the effect of the current when the Herradsvötn river is in flood.

The entrance to Siglufjord is very fine, and it is remarkable for its bold masses of lava. On the western side the flows are clearly indicated, as also is the peculiar erosion. There are bands of red tuff between some of the lava flows, also several scree slopes and alluvial fans at the foot ; on the eastern side there are pyramidal peaks. Inside the fjord and at its head the bold scenery is continued. All this was made brilliant by some wonderful sunset effects later in the evening.

CHAPTER XVIII

THE next port at which we touched was Akureyri in
Eyjafjord, the place from which we had started several
weeks before to cross the island. We arrived at
about nine in the morning, and the vessel was timed
to stay there two days before departing for Husavik.
I had formed the plan that if we reached Akureyri
in good time, I would make a two days' trip across
country to Husavik, and there pick up the steamer
again. Fortune favoured me, for on going on deck
to get a boat to take me ashore, where I intended
to hunt up a guide and ponies, I came face to face
with Sigurthur, one of our guides on the Akureyri-
Reykjavik journey. Sigurthur had just come aboard
to look for old friends. As he was disengaged as a
guide, a few minutes sufficed to arrange with him to
act as conductor, and to supply ponies, etc., for the
journey, and in a few more he was rowing back to
the shore to make arrangements.

After breakfast I went ashore to purchase some
provisions, etc., and an hour or so after mid-day, all
being ready, we started from the Hotel Akureyri with
four ponies: two were for riding, one was for the

packs, and there was a spare animal.   We proceeded
south along the shore of the fjord for about a mile,
and then, as the tide was low, we struck off at right
angles straight through the water, by that means
saving about an hour and a half that would have
been required to round the head of the fjord.   The

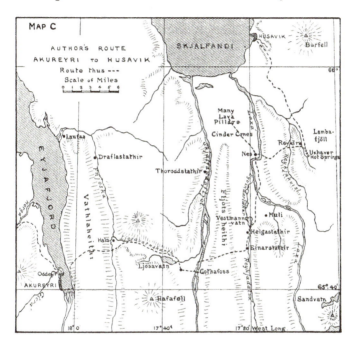

distance across was something between a mile and a
half and two miles; the water was rather deep in the
channels cut by the current from the river, and in
one the water reached to the saddle-flaps; but I
escaped a wetting by balancing myself on the saddle,
with feet tucked up.

On the eastern side of Eyjafjord we ascended the
steep side of Vathlaheithi by a long gradually-sloping

path to the top, whence we looked down upon Oddeyri, the suburb of Akureyri, whose formation has already been noted. A good view up the valley of the Eyjafjorthará was also obtained, showing the deltaic formation of the river where it enters the head of the fjord. From the top of Vathlaheithi there is a sharp descent by a zigzag road to the valley of the Fjnoská, an excellent specimen of a meandering river, on each side of which there are fine river-terraces. After crossing the river and ascending the terraces, we struck into Ljosavatnskarth. On the south side of this valley I came across a good example of various forms due to erosion. Below the upper lava flows there were some alluvial fans, and below that, cones and river-terraces. Just beyond, we passed along the northern shore of Ljosavatn, and proceeded to the farm-house of the same name, about a mile farther on, where we put up for the night.

When coming along the valley I learned the cause of what had sometimes struck me as strange. Towards evening I had often heard children uttering peculiar cries away up valley slopes, and I had imagined that they were calling to one another, but the real reason had never suggested itself to me : by their cries they were directing the dogs to "round up" and drive the milking-sheep to the farm-houses. Towards the end of the summer the sheep recognise the cries, and congregate without much rounding up by the dogs.

Next day was an interesting one, and we had fifteen hours in the saddle. Starting at eight in the morning, we did not get through to Husavik till eleven at night. The first point of interest on the day's journey was the Gothafoss, a fine waterfall on the

river Skjalfandafljot, which we reached after proceeding a few miles across some broken lava that was
partially covered by a deposit of clayey matter. The
fall is split into two main divisions by a hard dyke,
and it is probable that the rock on each side of it has
different degrees of hardness also, for the water flows
over at different levels. The central mass itself has
a depression in it, and a narrow stream of water runs
through it at much the same level as the higher of
the two big divisions. There is another fall a few
hundred yards lower down the river, but it is not so
impressive, and the height is only about one-fourth
that of the other. Just below the second fall, the
river is spanned by a bridge—a light wood and iron
structure supported on strong pillars built up from
the lava beneath. A few hundred yards below the
bridge there is a remarkably good example of river
erosion : the river has split at a hard dyke, which
stands in the middle of the stream resisting the rush
of the water.

From the bridge we made the gradual ascent to
Fljotsheithi, which we crossed, and then descended
into Reykjadalr to the farm-house of Einarstathir.
In a way, this day's journey was one of the most
annoying and tantalising of all I spent in Iceland.
Gun I had not, nor ammunition ; but I could have
counted grouse by the thousand, ducks by hundreds,
and golden plover by tens ! I could almost have
wept had there been time. I did not say very much
—if I had, the tears would have been apparent in my
voice ; but—I thought just about as deeply as the
sailor's parrot did. Fljotsheithi, over which we had
just come, had been alive with grouse ! Just think

of it—thousands of grouse, and—no gun! From
Einarsthathir we followed down the river Reykjadalsá
to Helgastathir, crossed it just beyond, and continued
down stream, past a number of lakes, the chief of
which is known as Vestmannsvatn. The Reykjadalsá
flows through these lakes; but from Vestmannsvatn
to its confluence with the Laxá it is known as
Eyvindarlaekur.

Just beyond Muli, which we left on our right, we
got upon lava again, and came to the Laxá, which
we crossed three times in the course of the day. We
made the first crossing at the spot where we first
touched it, and it proved to be the widest and
deepest fording-place in all the rivers I crossed in
Iceland. It was nearly half a mile wide, and I
entered without thinking it was very deep; but soon
I found otherwise, for the water often reached nearly
to the level of my knees. I was very anxious to get
across with dry feet, for it was comparatively early
in the day, and I knew that we had a long journey
before us. I had once suffered from the discomfort
of getting my boots filled with water and having to
ride for a considerable distance without change, so
did not wish to repeat the experience. By tucking up
my legs upon the saddle, and balancing somehow, I
did get over with dry feet, but my legs were fearfully
cramped on reaching the other side. My pony, however, did his best to give me a complete cold bath,
for he stumbled and went down on his knees in one
of the deepest spots; but I did not lose my balance,
and I succeeded in pulling him up without getting
more than just a few drops of water in one boot.
On we went over lava beside the Laxá for awhile,

but the river had to be recrossed a short distance
from Nes, a farm-house at which we pulled up for
lunch. Here we arranged for fresh ponies to take us
to a very fine lava-field a few miles to the north, and
induced the farmer to act as guide.

In the lava-field there were many examples of
circular vents, through which lava had spurted in

LAVA PILLARS NEAR NES.

times of volcanic activity. These vents were rounded
lava excrescences and circular pillars, all of which
were hollow inside. They were of somewhat similar
formation to two I saw in Vestri-Skarthsheithi on the
western side of Iceland, of which I took a photograph. The vegetation hereabouts is that common in
decomposing lava, and is chiefly birch scrub There
was an opening in the side of one of the largest vents,
through which I was able to crawl with my camera ;

unfortunately, I misjudged the light, so the negative
was much under-exposed, and the view of the interior
a complete failure.   The country about Nes is dotted
over with cones covered with cindery-looking scoria,
and having small central depressions; there are
hundreds of them, and all around they stick up above
the general level of the country.   All these cones
threw up more or less lava or cindery matter when
volcanic activity was in progress.

On our return to Nes we were met by the farmer's
wife, who informed us that during our absence *our*
ponies had got away and were then missing !   There
was a pretty mess !   What were we to do ?   Abandon
them, and go on with the farmer's ponies seemed to
be our only resource !   Time was pressing and
precious, for the light was failing, and to see the
Uxahver geysers was one of the objects of my expedition, and—we were still two hours distant from the
geysers !   While we were discussing the matter, we
were overjoyed to see the ponies suddenly come up
from between some of the farm outbuildings, followed
by the farmer's son, who had been in search of them.
We did not waste time then, but saddled up and
away ; but in less than a quarter of a mile we were
brought to a standstill by the river Laxá, at a spot
where we were to be ferried over.   Of course the
ferry-boat was not *there* ; it was some distance up the
river, and had to be sent for.   On its arrival, however,
there was no further delay, for we crossed at once, and
the ponies followed by swimming the river.   After
saddling up again we set off for Uxahver, taking
with us the farmer's son to show the shortest and
quickest way to the geysers.   We crossed Hvamsheithi

and forded the Reykjavisl and a smaller branch stream
on the way to Reykir farm-house.   On arrival there we
saw a quantity of steam rising from several places up
the valley, so we hastened towards the desired goal.
A stream of hot water runs down the valley from the
geysers, which are continually ejecting large volumes
of it : the stream's course is indicated by the light

UXAHVER GEYSER IN ERUPTION.

clouds of steam that rise from it.   We reached the
geysers at last, at about seven o'clock, in a bad and
failing light.   I proceeded at once to the chief of the
geysers, Uxahver, and got to work with my camera.
Uxahver very obligingly made one or two of its best
efforts, and I was fortunate to snap once or twice at
the right moment.   I also took a shot at it when
quiescent, with good result.   The next geyser of
importance, Bathstovukver, also gave an excellent

display that I took advantage of, and the resultant picture gives a better idea of a small geyser in eruption than any of the others.

When I had finished my shots at the geysers, Sigurthur informed me that we were then only about three hours distant from Husavik, where I had to pick up the steamer the next morning. It was not

BATHSTOVUKVER GEYSER IN ERUPTION.

quite eight o'clock, and the ponies seemed to be comparatively fresh after their rest in the middle of the day; so I thought it would be better, and Sigurthur agreed, to push on to Husavik, instead of staying at Reykir till the morning as we had originally intended when uncertain about procuring change ponies for part of the day's work. This arrangement would enable me to get on board without delay, if the weather should prove bad enough in the morning to prevent the *Vesta* from staying to take in cargo. At Husavik there is an open roadstead, and in stormy weather vessels do not remain long; sometimes they pass without calling at all. We *did* push on, and the farther we went the fresher the ponies seemed to get, until during the last hour they raced along at their best pace, evidently knowing their way and where they were going. The night was dark—*I* could not see the track, so I simply sat tight and let my pony go, without attempting to steer, trusting to him to make the best of the way; this he did at top speed without a single stumble the whole way—a feat that he had not accomplished in broad daylight. We arrived at the hotel at Husavik just at eleven o'clock, after fifteen hours in the saddle. In the earlier part of the day, Sigurthur had several times hinted that what I wanted to do could not be done in the time at our disposal; but I intended to try. So it happened that, with the aid of extra ponies and guides, and by dint of impressing Sigurthur with my determination, he gradually came round to the same view, and at last expressed agreement that it *might* be done if things went smoothly; from that time he made no further suggestion as to the desirableness of "cutting" some part of the journey, and we got through it all successfully.

I found the accommodation at the hotel quite good, and at breakfast an excellent meal was served. One of the dishes was "whale"—a thick gelatine kind of stuff, cut from the fin of the whale. I took a small piece and found it almost tasteless.

I have omitted previously to note that *skyr* is one of the articles of food served at all the farm-houses. It is a kind of clotted cream, eaten with powdered sugar, and milk or ordinary cream poured over it. At the hotel at Husavik the *skyr* was of the best quality, as indeed it was at most of the farms, though sometimes it had a distinctly peaty flavour that was due to the nature of the surrounding country. Another article of food in general use, which we obtained from time to time from the farmhouses, is a sort of flat pancake introduced by the Danes. It is of a very leathery nature, and we used to tear off pieces as we wanted it, though more often one took a piece of the stuff and offering a corner to another the two would pull it apart. In spite of its leathery qualities, when eaten with butter and jam, and with good appetite as sauce, it is not so bad

CHAPTER XIX

THE *Vesta* was late in arrival, and as the taking in of cargo occupied several hours, we did not get away from Husavik till the afternoon; we then headed straight for the Arctic Circle, passing the island of Lundey on the way out of Skjalfandi. When we entered within the Arctic Circle in the evening, the atmospheric conditions and the temperature were in keeping with our position on the earth's surface, for it was cold and bleak, and the night promised to be a dirty one; but the weather during the night was not so bad after all, and when I awoke in the morning it was to find the sunshine streaming into my cabin through the open port.

At Vopnafjord we remained from early morning till late at night. We climbed the hills at the back of the town and made our way over towards Nypsfjord. From an elevated spot we obtained a view looking into that fjord. It was not a scene of striking beauty, but I was interested to see that the entrance to the inner fjord was narrowed considerably by a spit that extended well into it, perhaps two-thirds across. This had been formed, as usual, by the sea beating in and banking up the detritus brought down by the river, the Vestradalsá. Up there on the rises I succeeded in stalking some sheep and in photographing them. I had tried several times before, but had always failed. Nearly all the sheep in Iceland are horned, while most of the cattle are without horns. There were several things of interest in Vopnafjord that I photographed—the interior of a cod-fish store being one of them; another was the home of "Socrates," a notification to that effect being prominent on the front of the house. There were several stores on a point near the middle of the town, and in front of them there were about a dozen fish-drying grids lying on the slope of the beach. Here at Vopnafjord we found the people to be most curious regarding us and our movements. It was Sunday, and having nothing to do, they displayed to the fullest extent the Icelander's worst characteristic, that of staring hard and persistently.

In the afternoon while cargo was being taken in, a little mild excitement was caused by the capsizing of nine bales of wool into the water, and by their subsequent rescue from drifting out to sea by a boat that went in pursuit.

Before departing from Vopnafjord we had an invasion of Icelanders. They came on board, boat-loads at a time; the smoking-room was soon full of them, and there were crowds on deck. I was writing in a recess just above the companion-way to the saloon; small crowds descended by it to the regions below and did not reappear—goodness knows where they managed to stow themselves. A fellow-

passenger came up from a visit to his cabin and
informed me that he had stumbled over two of the
Icelanders, who had taken possession of his cabin.
Helvit!—to use the mild Icelandic swear-word—
what about mine? I went down to see what was
going on in *my* cabin, and returned on deck breathing
more freely (in two ways!), for I found that my cabin
companion had early taken possession and had so
far kept out all invaders, in spite of repeated attacks
upon his stronghold. The atmosphere below was
becoming quite oppressive, and one could almost have
cut out a chunk of it!—hence, as I have stated, I
breathed more freely on deck. But it occurred to
me that if I took possession of my own bunk, I
could help my companion in resisting future attacks
of the enemy; so I went down again.

"There's a cry and a shout, and a deuce of a rout"
going on generally, for we had arrived at Seythisfjord,
and the invading horde was preparing to leave the
vessel—it had come to take part in the ceremony of
unveiling a monument that was to be performed that
day, and to enjoy the subsequent festivities and
gaieties. The trampling of feet above informed me
that the natives were congregating round the com-
panion-ladder. I shoved my head through the port-
hole, and there, but a few yards off, were two or three
boats. One was just pulling away very fully laden,
another was loading up with passengers, and a third
awaiting its turn to take on its human cargo. I went
to my tub, and so, for a few minutes, escaped from
the noise.

During breakfast I listened to the tales of woe as
related by my fellow-passengers. One had had four

of the natives camped in his cabin. In the morning
they severally made use of his sponge and soap in
performing their ablutions, while his tooth-brush only
just escaped service. Whatever of his effects were
lying loose about his cabin were subjected to inspection and examination : a bottle of " Elliman's " was
uncorked and smelt, and the Icelanders seemed
inclined to taste, but in their discretion refrained ;
had they but tested its virtues, they would no doubt
have found it a most excellent pick-me-up. After
performing his own toilet he went on deck, but on
returning to his cabin a few minutes later, found two
women in possession, and busy at his wash-basin.
My fellow-passenger was a man who did not object
to cleanliness in a general way, but for the native
Icelander, both sexes, to take possession of his cabin
and make use of his toilet things, was too much for
his nerves. If he did not take a leaf out of the
Icelanders' book and make use of their swear-word,
Helvit ! it was only because he was a clergyman ; but
I have no doubt that he thought that and much more
of a similar kind !

Another passenger reported that he had lost one
of his native companions in a very extraordinary way.
I must state that some of the Icelanders have the
disgusting habit of spitting in all sorts of places, and
they are not, as a rule, particular where—to them the
whole world is a spittoon ! This passenger stated that
he had found a big Icelander in his cabin the night
before, who remarked that he was going to sleep
there, and immediately afterwards made some noisy
throaty sounds, inquiring where he could spit. On
being informed that it was not customary for anybody

to spit anywhere in a cabin, and that there was no
place where *he* could do so, he looked surprised and
expressed himself to that effect.   Much to this
passenger's relief, the Icelander then took himself
off from the cabin, and was seen there no more.   No
doubt the native had found some spot where he was
able to indulge his habit to his heart's content.

I went ashore after breakfast, and landed just in
time to see a procession of Icelanders and others.
The occasion was the unveiling of a memorial stone
that had been erected by the inhabitants of Seythisfjord and the surrounding country to the memory of
a Norwegian, one Otto Andreas Wathue, who died in
1898.   This man had been instrumental in making
Seythisfjord a place of considerable importance, and
its prosperity was due entirely to him.

The ceremony had drawn to Seythisfjord all the
notabilities of the neighbourhood, as well as others
from the near fjords, and a few from such distant
places as Akureyri; it had also drawn thither two
Danish men-of-war, and there were in port three
vessels belonging to the United Steamship Company:
the *Ceres*, the *Vesta*, and another.   Some of the chief
of the officers from the war-ships attended in their
official capacity, while others from the Company's three
vessels also attended the ceremony; several joined in
the procession, which started from the veiled monument at the head of the fjord near the heart of the
town.   The Norwegian, Wathue, had lived on the south
side of the fjord in a large house about a mile from
the monument, and there the widow still lived.   The
procession made its way along the road by the side
of the fjord, and then passed the house, where every-

body saluted the widow, who, with her relatives and
a few friends, was a spectator from an elevated grass
plat.   I was standing just beside the house taking
snap-shots.   My picture shows the head of the
procession : some of the leading figures may be seen
in the act of saluting the party assembled on the
grass in front of the house.   The procession halted a

THE PROCESSION AT SEYTHISFJORD.

short distance beyond, and then returned to the
starting-point at the monument, round which the
members of it congregated.   The ceremony of unveiling was performed after some speechifying had been
got through and several poems, composed by Icelandic
poets for the occasion, had been recited or sung.
Those assembled then adjourned to the fête ground on
the other side of the river, where dancing and running

and other athletic sports were carried on during the
rest of the day, and where fireworks were displayed
in the evening. I took several photographs on the
outskirts of the crowd round the monument while the
ceremony of unveiling was going on; in them are
two young women attired in the national costume.
One is dressed in white and the other in a dark dress,

SEYTHISFJORD—ON THE OUTSKIRTS OF THE CROWD ROUND THE MONUMENT.

but both have on the peculiar national state head-
dress.

We called at Northfjord in the early morning, and
after less than an hour there, set sail for Eskefjord,
arriving there just before breakfast-time. Though we
remained for several hours, I did not get ashore, for
there was so much uncertainty about the time of
departure that we might have started at any moment;
there was also the usual difficulty of getting a boat.

Faskruthsfjord is a very picturesque place; bold and peculiarly shaped mountains are all around. A liparite and tuff mountain on the southern side is noticeable chiefly for the inclined strata that lie upon its southern slopes. Behind the town a huge pyramid (a fine example of the result of denudation) towers high above. Faskruthsfjord is the chief resort of the French fishermen who carry on their avocation on the coast of Iceland, and though there are a few Icelanders in the settlement, yet the greater number are French.

During the latter part of the voyage we had a passenger, an Englishwoman, lying dangerously ill. The doctor from ashore, an Icelander, came on board here to see her, as other doctors had at other ports of call; but he did not go away decently as the others had—no, he remained on board drinking and smoking, and talking at the top of his voice, with a number of men from shore, the carousal being carried on just outside the cabin-door of his patient! A specimen of the customs of the country as observed by at least *one* Icelander!

Our last port of call in Iceland was in Berufjord, where we arrived at about six in the morning. As it was rainy and misty, I could not well judge of the scenery. It looked an interesting place, and there were several sharp conical peaks showing dimly through the thick atmosphere. We put to sea about an hour later, in weather that promised to be blowy, and the promise was fulfilled, for we were soon in a fairly heavy sea, which increased as the day wore on; it continued bad until we approached the Faroes next day, when it cleared up, and we had bright, fine weather while amongst those islands.

We obtained excellent views of the various headlands at the north end of the Faroes ; it was noticeable
that all had perpendicular precipices facing the north,
where the sea is continually at work eroding their
bases. We passed through Kalsofjord, the channel
between the island of Kalso on the west and those of
Kuno and Bordo on the east. The islands have many
corries, soft dykes, and mountains of pyramidal shape.
There are several villages most picturesquely situated
in the valleys and corries, but as we steamed along in
mid channel we were not near enough for the camera
to be of service.

We reached Thorshavn in the early afternoon, so I
went ashore for an hour to have another look at the
picturesque town and at the Faroese. In the evening
we set sail for Leith.

FAREWELL FAROESE !

APPENDIX I

NOTES ON PLANTS COLLECTED IN THE FAROES AND ICELAND

By A. W. HILL, M.A.

THE decumbent character of the vegetation and the practical absence of trees form the most striking features of the flora in both the Faroes and Iceland. In the Faroes the steep and rocky hillsides are very exposed and wind swept, and the vegetation is in consequence characteristically dwarfed, and most plants raise themselves but little above the general level of the grass.

The dwarfed habit was well shown by some plants, such as *Orchis maculata*, which was very common on the slopes, and was only a few inches high. The inflorescences did not, as a rule, bear more than five to ten flowers, which, however, were large and pale in colour. The ovaries in many cases were not twisted, so that the labellum was consequently uppermost.

Another example of the effect of the conditions on the vegetation was afforded by the dandelion *Taraxacum dens leonis*, which exhibited the prostrate habit exceedingly well, for in order to protect the flowers from the wind, the flower scapes were bent over and laid parallel to the surface of the ground and the inflorescence was exposed to the light by a right-angled bend of the scape just below the head of the flowers. The inflorescence was by this means protected from the wind by being kept just below the general level of the vegetation.

Cardamine pratensis was also influenced in a similar way on the lower slopes, but at higher altitudes plants were found bearing single radical flowers on short stalks instead of the usual raceme.

217

We proceeded to Akureyri in the north of Iceland by way of the east coast, and it was interesting to notice the difference in the condition of the vegetation on the northern and eastern shores of the island. On the east coast, at Seythis- and Vopna-fjords, the plants were stunted and for the most part only in bud ; but in the north, at Husavik and Akureyri, similar plants were much earlier, and were not only in full flower, but were also much less stunted, and showed a more robust growth than those found on the eastern side. For example, *Plantanthera hyperborea*, which was in tight bud on the east coast, and also *Thymus* and other plants, were in full flower at Husavik.

Thalictrum alpinum, which grows abundantly all over the hillsides, was found to be attacked by the æcidial stage of one of the rust fungi, *Puccinia septentrionalis* ;[1] and at Seythisfjord, where it was especially noticed, it was found that only the top-most leaflets were affected, that is to say, only those leaflets which protruded above the general level of the vegetation, and which were in consequence infected by wind-blown spores. At Seythisfjord the leaflets were only slightly attacked, the fungus being in a young state ; but at Husavik it was much more advanced, and the hypertrophied purple tissues were very conspicuous. The effect often extended some way down the petioles.

The case of the fungus is a further example of the greater forwardness of the plants in the north.

There can be no doubt that the characteristics of the east coast vegetation are due to the prevalence of cold winds and the occurrence of cold currents.

Whilst crossing the island several interesting features of the vegetation were noticed. Between Akureyri and our first camp (Thverá) several "forests" were passed through, consisting of *Betula nana, Vaccinium uliginosum*, and Willows, *Salix lanata* and *S. glauca* rising to a height of from nine to eighteen inches, with an undergrowth of other small plants.

The hillsides all round were covered by *Dryas octopetala*, which was by far the commonest plant in the northern half of the island, and it was abundant also on the east coast.

Travelling along the Oxnadal and then turning off towards Silfrastathir, *Dryas* at first was the most conspicuous feature of the vegetation covering the rocky moraines and talus slopes ; but about three miles from the head of the valley the *Dryas*

---

[1] *Polygonum viviparum* is the "host" for the Uredo stage of this fungus, and the disease was noticed on it in several places.

was replaced by *Cerastium alpinum* and *Potentilla maculata,* which then in their turn became the dominant plants for a considerable distance. As we traversed the island we kept passing through well-marked zones of different plants, whose limits seemed largely to be determined by the character of the soil.

After crossing the " col " some very rough screes were passed, on which the Iceland poppy, *P. nudicaule,* was growing abundantly. The screes were formed of rough angular blocks with very little soil between them, and the poppy was only growing in the most barren spots ; where moraines occurred the poppy did not grow. It was also found on the stony ground by the river at Silfrastathir.

The hillsides were covered in many places by large tracts of *Equisetum* (*E. arvense* and *E. pratense*). The various species of the Equisetaceæ seem to be among some of the commonest plants of the island. The swampy regions by the rivers are covered with *Equisetum* and *Scirpus cæspitosus ;* and they are very abundant on the mountains.

From the river until we reached Gilhagi, the flora showed no features of any particular note ; but a meadow there with large plants of *Saxifraga cernua* in full flower was a very beautiful sight.

On ascending from Gilhagi a change in the flora was gradually seen. After about 2000 feet *Pedicularis flammea* appeared and became common ; on the lower slopes the leaves were green and the plants tall, but at greater elevations the plants became short and stunted, with deep red leaves. The high ground was very much broken up, being of a deep hummocky character and covered by a dwarfed growth of Willows, *Empetrum,* Mosses, etc.

Passing over ground from which the snow had just melted, the willows were found to be either still quite bare or just coming out into leaf, but everywhere in such barren places cones of *Equisetum* were seen sticking up on pale brown stalks some six inches above the soil; the sterile green shoots do not grow up until some time after the appearance of the cones.

All around Athalmansvatn the ground was very hummocky, the mounds being from a foot to eighteen inches high, with narrow depressions or ruts between. The elevation of this region was about 2500 feet, and as the snow had only recently melted, everything was in consequence backward, *Thalictrum* and willows, etc., not yet being in flower.

Leaving Athalmansvatn a large tract of hummocky ground was crossed, covered chiefly by *Cassiope hypnoides, Empetrum,*

Willows, *Salix lanata* and *S. herbacea*, Grey Lichens, such as *Cladonia*, and Mosses. After this our route lay across a piece of the northern desert land or *Sandr*, which is a barren, sandy, and stony expanse. The soil was a light brownish loam, and was easily blown about by the wind, and scattered all over it were large angular or rounded blocks of stone. *Arabis petræa* was the only plant occurring in any quantity over this region, and it formed a very conspicuous feature in the landscape, growing in rosettes closely adpressed to the soil with the racemes of flowers growing out horizontally.

As we travelled on in a southerly direction, *Silene acaulis* appeared and then a little thrift, *Armeria sibirica*, and the *Arabis* became less frequent. Here the soil was more sandy, and the strong wind blew clouds of dust. Still farther south, *Armeria* reigned supreme over the desert; but occasional patches containing *Silene acaulis*, *Potentilla*, *Cerastium alpinum*, and *Silene maritima* occurred. Where the soil became more loamy, *Arabis petræa* again came in. At the edge of the desert the willows were seen encroaching on the sand, and soon a willow and birch (*Betula nana*) scrub was passed through, which in its turn gave place to moister land with *Empetrum*, *Pedicularis flammea*, etc.

Near Blandá, *Salix phyllicifolia* was noticed for the first time. A good deal of hummocky ground was also passed over, and its characteristic and invariable features were noticed (*v.* later).

After passing over very rough morainic ground with snow still lying in patches and quite devoid of vegetation, we reached Hveravellir, a perfect oasis in the desert. The hot springs and fumaroles occur along a long line of fissure, and warm up the soil of a considerable tract of country in their neighbourhood. The effect on the vegetation is most striking, for a strip of verdant meadow-land occurs in the middle of bare country, covered in many places with snow at the end of June. All the flowers occurring there were in a very forward state, and a large number of different plants were obtained; some spots were yellow with buttercups, and the ground was carpeted with thyme in full bloom.

Botrychium lunaria occurred in quantity, and a very small variety of *Ophioglossum vulgatum*, *O. vulgatum*, var. *polyphyllum*, was found in a warm place. *Selaginella spinosa* was also abundant.

On the edges of this warm tract barren land occurred and in many places snow, so that there was a very sharp contrast between the warm and cold earth; and on the latter the willows were only just coming into leaf.   This tract of country occurs at the edge of the great lava flow from Strytur.

Towards   Strytur   the   lava   was   in   places   covered   by " hummocky ground," which showed the usual features noticed elsewhere.

The characteristic plants seem invariably to be :—

* *Carex vulgaris (rigida)*, a creeping variety.
* *Salix lanata.*
* *Salix herbacea.*
* *Cassiope hypnoides.*
* *Empetrum nigrum* (very abundant).
* *Vaccinium uliginosum.*
  Loiseleuria procumbens.
  Armeria sibirica.
  Silene acaulis (not very frequent).
  Bartsia alpina.
  Pedicularis flammea.
* Two or three Lichens, species of *Cladonia*, and a Moss, *Rhacomitrium lanuginosum.*

Those marked with an asterisk appear to be invariably present, the others are not so constant, but some are usually found.

Shortly   after   leaving   Hveravellir   the   watershed   of   the island was crossed, and a marked difference in the flora was noticed in the valley, Thjofadal, on the southern side of the ridge, owing no doubt to the much greater rainfall which occurs on this, the south-western, side of the island.

Among plants noticed in this region, which had not been met with before, were :—

  Draba alpina.
  Cardamine bellidifolia, and
  Ranunculus pygmæus (which grew upright in the valley, but was prostrate and creeping on the surrounding hillsides).

Fungoid diseases were very prevalent in the valley, and *Saxifraga cæspitosa*, which was extremely dwarfed on the high ridges, was in many places badly attacked by a rust fungus.

Saxifraga cernua was also affected by the conditions in this region, for in other localities north of the watershed all the plants were found with the usual terminal flower, but here no terminal flower was developed, and the upright stems bore leaves and bulbils only.

Epilobium latifolium occurred among the stones in the glacier streams, and a very decumbent form of *Epilobium alpinum* was common on the hillsides.

The hills all round were formed of loose morainic matter, the slopes consisting of fine sandy earth with pebbles, and the vegetation is distributed on the hillsides in the form of banks and terraces, thus giving the hills a peculiar appearance with very gentle steps. In some cases the vegetation has spread and grown over the edges of the terraces, and by further growth hummocks have been formed.

The formation of hummocky ground on a morainic hillside appears to be somewhat as follows:—

If conditions, such as snow-line, wind, etc. (on a bare hillside of sandy and stony ground) permit, isolated plants begin to appear, and collect soil around them by their prostrate habit of growth and with their roots; in consequence of the loose nature of the soil, and owing to the action of snow or water, slipping frequently takes place, and the plants tend to keep up the earth. As the plants spread, terraces get formed and the plants bank up the loose earth, and the mountain-side is then broken up into broad steps. The vegetation continues to grow over the edges of the terraces, and in consequence more soil is collected by the plants, and small mounds result, and later on, if the slope is not too great, true hummocks may be formed. If the slope is steep, the hummocks are usually flat-topped, but this is also often due to snow, wind, etc.

The hummocky ground usually seen occurs in fairly level country, and its origin may probably have been somewhat different from that just described; the hummocks are from one to two feet high, and the ruts between are often so narrow that two hummocks have frequently united. The normal breadth of a hummock is from one to two feet across, and it is closely covered by *Empetrum* or *Cassiope*, with *Carex vulgaris*, the Moss *Rhacomitrium lanuginosum*, and the other plants already enumerated.

Hummocky ground was also met with in meadows at Gilhagi (near Maelifell); here they were covered by grass and other meadow-plants, and *Saxifraga cernua* grew in masses in the depressions. These hummocks were on a hillside, and may have been originally formed in the manner already described; but owing to some change in the snow-line, meadow-land plants may have wandered up the hillside, and ousted the characteristic plants of the hummocks.

Our journey from Thjofadal to Gránanes lay for the most part over the lava-flows from Strytur, which were covered by a close-growing vegetation, large tussocks of moss, very dwarf *Saxifrages*,

S. cæspitosa, Empetrum, Salix herbacea, and other plants usually found on the hummocks. True hummocks were, however, rare.

Near our camp and before the Svatá was reached we came to the end of the lava and crossed a sandy tract, and the usual change in the flora was at once noticeable; large clumps of willows bound the sand together, around which the soil collected, forming mounds, and patches of *Armeria, Arabis petræa, Silene,* and *Arenaria* were scattered about. In some places the willows were killed by having been buried in the blown sand.

Between Gránanes and Hvitarvatn the country is at first hummocky, and then covered by birch and willow scrub. On the hummocks, especially in the patches of moss, *Saxifraga Hirculus* was not uncommon. The large tract of swampy ground at the edge of the lake was covered by masses of cotton grass. Leaving Hvitarvatn our way lay through willow scrub until the Hvitá was reached. After crossing the river the ground was very rough, being composed of morainic matter from the adjacent mountains and covered with large angular blocks of lava. The only flowers growing here were *Arenaria, Armeria, Thymus* and *Dryas* in isolated patches. As we travelled farther south, the plants were noticed to be taller and more vigorous than those seen in the interior, and the flora was more home-like in character. *Juniperus, Betula odorata, Calluna,* and *Arctostaphylos uva ursi* were noticed for the first time.

Both birches (*B. odorata, B. nana*) were very plentiful, and from two to three feet high (in the north *B. nana* was only six to nine inches high) willows were not common.

Between Sandá and Gullfoss another small desert area was traversed where earth-pillars occurred. The plants were hardly able to exist, as the smaller ones were blown away, and the willows and birches were in many places buried by the blown sand.

Around Gullfoss the vegetation was luxuriant, *Geum rivale, Geranium sylvaticum,* and *Alchemilla vulgaris* covered the ground, and above *Rubus saxatilis* and *Fragaria vesca* were abundant, whilst *Arctostaphylos uva ursi* also grew in profusion.

At Bratholt we reached civilisation again, and were presented with some of the lichen from which the orange dye, still used in the island, is obtained.

Between Geysir and Thingvellir we passed through one of the largest forests in the island; the hillsides were covered with birch-bushes, and in places they were quite six feet high; usually they did not rise to a height of more than three or four feet, and the topmost branches became entangled in our legs as we rode among the bushes. All four species of birch were noticed, and the scent of the bruised leaves was very pleasant. By way of undergrowth, the ground was carpeted with *Geranium sylvaticum*, *Ranunculus repens*, and large patches of *Orchis maculata*, etc. It was altogether a beautiful spot, and we spent nearly four hours wending our way through it. The river Bruará runs through the middle of this forest.

At Thingvellir *Gentiana nivalis* was found among other plants. The rarity of blue flowers in the part of the island visited by us, and indeed throughout the island, was very striking, as the only other blue flowers noticed, besides the gentian, were the *Veronicas*, and the *Myosotis* and *Viola tricolor* found at Akureyri, and *Campanula rotundifolia* and *Pleurogyne rotata*, which were found on the east coast on the return journey. *Gentiana campestris* and *G. nivalis* were also found on the west coast. *White, pale pink*, and *yellow* were the common colours, white being the predominant. The three most common orchids, *Habenaria albida*, *Habenaria viridis*, and *Plantanthera hyperborea* were green and fairly inconspicuous. Perhaps the most striking flowers are the large rose-coloured *Epilobium latifolium*, which grows on bare islands of stones and black sand in the glacier streams, the yellow *Saxifraga Hirculus*, and *Dryas octopetala*, which covers vast tracts of country.

Between Thingvellir and Reykjavik is an extensive *Heithi*, over which we rode rapidly. There appeared to be no features of any special interest, and as the day was very wet it was not possible to study the flora carefully. On the beach at Reykjavik *Mertensia maritima* is a fairly common plant.

The hot springs at Hveravellir and other places contain large quantities of algæ, mostly belonging to the blue-green family or *Cyanophyceæ*. Specimens were collected from various springs at Hveravellir, Kerlingarfjöll, and Geysir, and the temperature of the water in which they were growing was carefully recorded. As I was unable to examine them in detail, I sent them to Professor West of Cirencester, who has worked through my material and published a paper on hot-spring algæ in the *Journal of Botany*,[1] in which he gives a list of all the algæ we brought back from Iceland.

---

[1] "On some Algæ from Hot Springs," G. S. West, *Journal of Botany*, July 1902, p. 242.

The highest temperature at which algæ were found was 85° C. (185° F.). Most of the forms found had not been previously recorded from Iceland, and there was one new species belonging to the genus *Aulosira*, *A. thermalis*. Full details of these interesting algæ will be found in the paper to which a reference has been given.

Q

APPENDIX II

A LIST OF PLANTS COLLECTED IN THE FAROES AND ICELAND IN JUNE AND JULY 1900

Caltha palustris . .	I.	F.
Ranunculus flammula .		F.
hyperboreus . .	I.	Seythisfjord, Kerlingarfjöll.
pygmæus . . .	I.	Thjofadal.
repens . . .	I.	F.
Thalictrum alpinum . .	I.	F.
Papaver nudicaule . .	I.	Near Silfrastathir on screes and among stones in river bed.
Arabis alpina . . .	I.	Thjofadal.
petræa . . .	I.	The desert between Athalmansvatn and Hveravellir, near Gránanes.
Cardamine bellidifolia .	I.	Thjofadal.
pratensis . . .	I.	F.
Cochlearia officinalis . .	I.	F.
grœnlandica . .	I.	
Draba alpina . . .	I.	Thjofadal.
rupestris . . .	I.	
verna . . .	I.	F.
incana . . .	I.	Silfrastathir, etc.
tomentosa . .	I.	

Viola ericetorum	. .	I.	F.
palustris .	. .	I.	F.
tricolor .	. .	I. Akureyri.	
Polygala vulgaris	. .		F.
Alsine arctica[1] .	. .	I. Athalmansvatn, Thjofadal.	
Cerastium alpinum	.	I.	
trigynum .	. .	I. Akureyri.	
triviale .	. .	I.	
Halianthus peploides	.		F. Klaksvig.
Lychnis flos cuculi	. .		F.
Silene acaulis .	. .	I.	F.
Silene maritima	. .	I.	
Lychnis alpina .	. .	I.	
Stellaria uliginosa	. .	I. Seythisfjord.	
Arenaria norvegica	. .	I.	
rubella .	. .	I.	
Montia fontana	. .	I.	F.
Hypericum pulchrum	.		F. Klaksvig.
Linum catharticum .	.	I.	
Geranium sylvaticum	.	I.	F.
Vicia cracca .	. .	I. Narfeyri.	
Alchemilla alpina	. .	I.	F.
vulgaris .	. .	I.	F.
Comarum palustre	. .	I.	F.
Dryas octopetala	. .	I.	F.
Geum rivale .	. .	I.	F.
Fragaria vesca .	. .	I.	
Potentilla anserina	. .	I. Reykholt.	
maculata .	. .	I.	
tormentilla	. .	I.	F.
Rubus saxatilis	. .	I. Modruvellir, Gullfoss, etc.	
Sibbaldia procumbens	.	I. Athalmansvatn, Hveravellir.	
Hippuris vulgaris	. .	I.	

[1] Not in *Warming's* list, but given by *Babington* from Akureyri.

Epilobium alpinum	. .	I.	Thjofadal.
latifolium .	. .	I.	Gránanes.
palustre .	. .	I.	
alsinefolium	. .	I.	Kerlingarfjöll.

Rhodiola rosea .	. .	I.	Thjofadal.	
Sedum villosum	. .	I.		

Saxifraga aizoides	. .	I.	Vopnafjord.	
cernua	. .	I.	Gilhagi and Thjofadal.	
cæspitosa .	. .	I.		F.
Hirculus .	. .	I.		
hypnoides	. .	I.		
nivalis	. .	I.		
oppositifolia	. .	I.		
rivularis .	. .	I.	Thjofadal, Sandá, etc.	
stellaris .	. .	I.		F.
Parnassia palustris .	.	I.	Hveravellir, near Springs, etc.	

Angelica sylvestris .	.	I.	
Hydrocotyle vulgaris	.	I.	

Galium boreale	. .	I.		
uliginosum	. .	I.		F.

Achillea millefolium .	.	I.		F.
Bellis perennis .	. .	I.		F.
Erigeron alpinus	. .	I.		
Gnaphalium norvegicum	.	I.	Isafjord, Hveravellir.	
supinum .	. .	I.	Isafjord, Hveravellir.	
Taraxacum dens leonis	.	I.		F.

Campanula rotundifolia	.	I.	Vopnafjord, Seythisfjord.

Pyrola media .	. .	I.	Hveravellir, Sandá.
Vaccinium uliginosum	.	I.	
Arctostaphylos uva ursi	.	I.	Near Thingvellir.
Cassiope hypnoides .	.	I.	(Especially on hummocky ground.)
Calluna vulgaris	.	I.	Near Thingvellir.
Loiseleuria procumbens	.	I.	Seythisfjord,Athalmansvatn.

Pinguicula vulgaris   .   .   I.   Hveravellir, near Springs. F.

Gentiana campestris .   .   I.   Helgafell.
    nivalis   .   .   .   I.   Thingvellir.
Pleurogyne rotata   .   .   I.   Vopnafjord.
Menyanthes trifoliata   .   I.   Vopnafjord, etc.
Mertensia maritima .   .   I.   Reykjavik.
Myosotis arvensis   .   .   I.   Akureyri.
    versicolor .   .   .   F.

Bartsia alpina .   .   .   I.   (On hummocky ground.)
Euphrasia officinalis et. varr.   I.   F.
Pedicularis flammea .   .   I.   Gilhagi, Athalmansvatn.
Rhinanthus minor   .   .   I.   Sandá.
Veronica alpina   .   .   I.
    saxatilis .   .   .   I.
    serpyllifolia   .   .   I.   F.
    officinalis .   .   .   I.

Thymus serpyllum   .   .   I.   F.
Galeopsis tetrahit   .   .   I.   Geysir.
Prunella vulgaris   .   .   I.   Grund.

Armeria sibirica   .   .   I.

Plantago maritima   .   .   I.

Konigia islandica   .   .   I.
Oxyria digyna .   .   .   I.
Polygonum viviparum   .   I.
Rumex acetosa .   .   .   I.
    acetosella .   .   .   I.

Empetrum nigrum   .   .   I.

Salix glauca   .   .   .   I.
    herbacea .   .   .   I.   F.
    lanata   .   .   .   I.
    phyllicifolia   .   .   I.   S.W. Iceland.
    arctica   .   .   .   I.
    and others, hybrids,
      etc., which could not
      be determined.

Betula nana . , . I.
  alpestris . . . I.
  intermedia . . I.
  odorata . . . I.

Triglochin palustre . . I.
Corallorhiza innata . . I. Vopnafjord and Husavik.
Habenaria viridis . . I.   F.
  albida . . . I.
Orchis maculata . . I.   F.
Plantanthera hyperborea . I.

Tofieldia borealis . . I.

Juncus balticus . . I.
  trifidus . . . I.
Luzula campestris . . I.
  multiflora. . . I.
  spicata . . . I.

Scirpus cæspitosus . I.
Carex capillaris . . I.
  rigida . . . I.
  vulgaris . . . I. (Common on hummocky ground.)
Elyna spicata . . . I.
Eriophorum capitatum . I.
  angustifolium . . I.

Agrostis stolonifer . . I. Hveravellir.
Aira alpina . . . I.
Elymus arenarius . . I. Skagastrond.
Festuca ovina . . . I.
Hierochloe borealis . . I.
Phleum alpinum . . I.
Poa alpina . . . I.
Anthoxanthum odoratum . I.

Juniperus communis, v. nana I. Near Thingvellir.

Selaginella spinosa . . I. Hveravellir, etc.
Lycopodium alpinum . I. Hveravellir.   F.
  selago . . , I.

Blechnum spicant	.	.	F.
Cystopteris fragilis	.	.	I.
Botrychium lunaria	.	.	I.
Ophioglossum vulgatum, var. polyphyllum	.	I.	Hveravellir.
Equisetum arvense	.	.	I.
pratense	.	.	I.

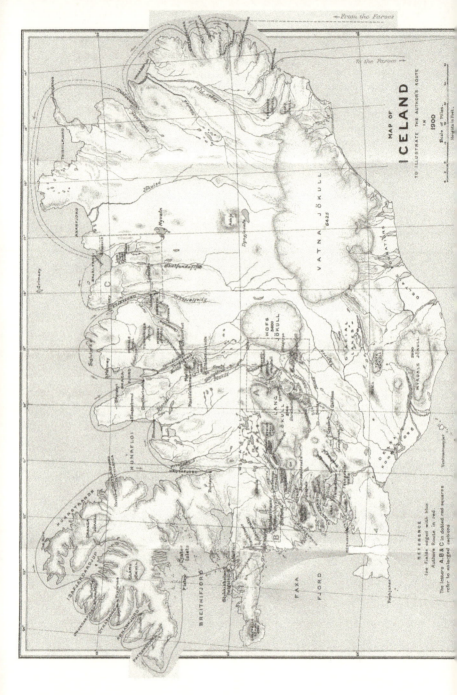

The material originally positioned here is too large for reproduction in this reissue. A PDF can be downloaded from the web address given on page iv of this book, by clicking on 'Resources Available'.

INDEX OF PLACES

THE END

Printed by R. & R. CLARK, LIMITED, *Edinburgh.*

For EU product safety concerns, contact us at Calle de José Abascal, 56–1°, 28003 Madrid, Spain or eugpsr@cambridge.org.